T0301709

Dialogue with China

Opportunities and Risks

Series on Dialogue with China

Series Editors: Stephan Rothlin *(Rothlin Ltd, Beijing, China & Rothlin Ltd, Hong Kong)*
Dennis P McCann *(Rothlin Ltd, Beijing, China & Rothlin Ltd, Hong Kong)*

Published:

Dialogue with China
Opportunities and Risks

Editors

Stephan Rothlin
Rothlin Ltd, Beijing, China & Rothlin Ltd, Hong Kong
Macau Ricci Institute at the University of St. Joseph, Macau

Dennis McCann
Rothlin Ltd, Beijing, China & Rothlin Ltd, Hong Kong

Mike Thompson
Gustavson School of Business, University of Victoria, Canada

World Scientific

NEW JERSEY · LONDON · SINGAPORE · BEIJING · SHANGHAI · HONG KONG · TAIPEI · CHENNAI · TOKYO

Published by

World Scientific Publishing Co. Pte. Ltd.
5 Toh Tuck Link, Singapore 596224
USA office: 27 Warren Street, Suite 401-402, Hackensack, NJ 07601
UK office: 57 Shelton Street, Covent Garden, London WC2H 9HE

Library of Congress Cataloging-in-Publication Data
Names: Rothlin, Stephan, 1959– editor. | McCann, Dennis, 1945– editor. |
 Thompson, Mike, 1958– editor.
Title: Dialogue with China : opportunities and risks / [edited by] Stephan Rothlin,
 Rothlin Ltd, Beijing, China & Rothlin Ltd, Hong Kong, Macau Ricci Institute at the
 University of St. Joseph, Macau; Dennis McCann, Rothlin Ltd, Beijing, China &
 Rothlin Ltd, Hong Kong; Mike Thompson, University of Victoria, Canada.
Description: New Jersey : World Scientific, [2022] | Series: Series on dialogue with China ; vol. 1 |
 Includes bibliographical references and index.
Identifiers: LCCN 2021052499 | ISBN 9789811248740 (hardcover) |
 ISBN 9789811250231 (ebook) | ISBN 9789811250200 (ebook other)
Subjects: LCSH: China--Economic conditions--2000- | China--Economic policy--2000– |
 Investments, Foreign--Government policy--China. | International business enterprises--China. |
 Commercial law--China.
Classification: LCC HC427.95 .D46 2022 | DDC 330.951--dc23/eng/20211228
LC record available at https://lccn.loc.gov/2021052499

British Library Cataloguing-in-Publication Data
A catalogue record for this book is available from the British Library.

Cover pictures by Klaus Pichler, Aastrasse 13, CH-8853 Lachen Switzerland;
Telephone: +41 55 442 55 94, Mobile: +41 79 419 61 78; http://www.pichlerphoto.ch.

For any available supplementary material, please visit
https://www.worldscientific.com/worldscibooks/10.1142/12598#t=suppl

Desk Editors: Balasubramanian Shanmugam/Pui Yee Lum

Typeset by Stallion Press
Email: enquiries@stallionpress.com

Printed in Singapore

Preface

Dialoguing with China sounds like an oxymoron. Trade conflicts, mutual apprehension, deep seated prejudices seem to be so pervasive that any attempt for in-depth communication and dialogue seems doomed to fail. Even people who have made a serious attempt to get a basic understanding of China seem at times lost in trying to cope with a country which considers itself again strongly at the Center of the World "中国", "*Zhong Guo*," which in so many ways seems to be at loggerheads with other cultures and countries. Although Chinese have become a familiar feature in every corner of the world thanks to the easing of travel restrictions for middle-class Chinese tourists this phenomenon has hardly contributed to a better mutual appreciation of cultures. In fact, the perceived insensitive performance of Chinese tourists all over the world has worried even the Chinese government. It may therefore come as no surprise for travelers going to China to watch videos in the subways sponsored by the Chinese government designed to urge their compatriots with practical examples to be more considerate of the values of other cultures especially in countries with a Moslem background.

The present series on "Dialogue with China" aims precisely to respond to this reality of mutual incomprehension. The purpose of the series is strongly focused on the attempt to analyze these barriers to understanding in order to remove them. These volumes are designed as consulting handbooks to help both academics and practitioners to engage in an educational adventure which would help them in their understanding and in their dealing with China. The different approaches to China and to the Chinese could be decisive in the process of earning full mutual trust, which seems to be crucial for successful business deals.

Different perspectives and arguments are discussed by outstanding experts in the field with a special concern that they are accessible to key decision-makers. As there is the constant risk of biased and opinionated statements by scholars from China and the West, it seems necessary that both players are challenged to express their views together in a profoundly Confucian attitude of self-criticism always making sure that common simplistic and disingenuous statements which do not respect the other party may consistently be avoided.

A particular challenge of a serious dialogue with China is the Herculean task of coming to grips with its 5,000 plus years history. However, it seems just necessary to constantly go back and forth between the different centuries and millennia on a macro-level in order not to lose sight and purpose within the myriads of apparently diverging phenomena but also to make every possible effort to understand properly the micro-level of a growing civil society including the amazing testimony of missionaries who ventured among the first travelers into totally unchartered waters. A particular breakthrough in the growing understanding of Chinese culture has been through Jesuit missionaries on the Silk Road, particularly Matteo Ricci (1552–1610) who in the 16th century recognized in his life-long ascent from Macau towards the Capital of the Middle Kingdom the pearl of great price inspiring their missionary drive. There are still lessons to be learnt from the achievements and struggles of these early adventurers along the Silk Road who never became discouraged in their genuine love for China. No matter how bitter the disappointments and frustrations may have been along a road which was always quite bumpy and along sea routes which were risky, these early pioneers seemed never to give up on their desire to learn from the Chinese and overcome mutual misunderstandings.

The main objective for this series is to address the needs of business practitioners, students, and instructors. As a result, there will be constant references and different types of analysis of China's Belt and Road Initiative (BRI) and the challenges involved in making it work to the mutual benefit of China and its partners in the BRI. The overall aim of the series is to stimulate reflection and critical inquiry among different actors both inside and outside China, on key factors indispensable for achieving successful collaboration in partnerships involving representatives of diverse backgrounds. In the case of the BRI, it is an ambitious and innovative attempt by the Chinese government to reach out to business people and representatives of other nations, requiring both knowledge and understanding of cultures that must be respected, if negotiations on specific BRI projects are to be successful and sustainable over the long run.

The handbooks featured in this series aim to inform parties both inside and outside China about the practical challenges in negotiating with culturally diverse partners. It very often appears in failed joint ventures that the amazing labyrinth of conditions for successful cooperation and the immensely rich web of trustworthy relations have been vastly underestimated and neglected. A central issue in each of the books in this series concerns the nature of the diversity of China's own cultural traditions. These will create opportunities for dialogue in good faith, thereby establishing the trust required for sustainable collaboration. Conversely, China's prospective partners will be challenged to understand how their own commitments and perspectives may converge toward productive dialogue and mutual trust. Each of the books will also reflect on various aspects of this challenge in light of the BRI's initial developments, what has worked and what has not, in understanding and deploying the cultural dimensions of the BRI agenda.

The series that Rothlin Ltd, the Macau Ricci Institute and the University of Saint Joseph, Macau, is proposing is based on more than two decades of experience promoting cultural exchanges between the East and the West as well as corporate social responsibility in and with China. A key lesson from many mixed experiences is that sustainable business success presupposes positive moral engagement and mutual appreciation of the role of values — emergent from the wisdom traditions of various cultures — in shaping our attitudes toward business and economics. Consistent with China's Confucian moral philosophy, success in business and economics can only be sustained on an adequate understanding of morality and ethics as well as on the spiritualities that support them.

Given the practical focus of this series, the contributors have adopted a relatively easy and readable writing style without too many academic references which should enable many people, for whom English is a second language, to cope with a most complex cross-cultural environment. Both Chinese and Western scholars will create concrete roadmaps for negotiating key areas of the BRI such as practical ethics, cross-cultural literacy, environmental responsibility, as well as wisdom traditions and religions. Authors have been invited based on their ability to demonstrate an awareness of the cross-cultural conditions of the BRI.

The first book in the series opens the discussion of how to dialogue with China, by featuring a selection of articles published in the *Macau Ricci Institute Journal* (MRIJ) in its first six issues from 2017 through 2020. The bilingual journal is dedicated to promoting an enlightened dialogue with China by focusing on three core dimensions, namely: Comparative Spirituality, Moral Leadership, and Social Innovation. While these three dimensions are featured in each issue of the Journal, the following essays have been selected for inclusion in this introductory volume, because of the series' focus on China's diversity of its cross-cultural traditions.

Another complex inquiry will explore the philosophies of governance and statecraft operative in the diverse cultures. The aim is to increase understanding of the norms, both tacit and explicit, that provide the operative assumption for how successful negotiations can be conducted and projects successfully completed. Managing expectations with well-informed understanding is the key to cross-cultural cooperation.

Another main focus will be on the diversity of ethical traditions, enabling the reader to make comparisons, find convergences, and achieve mutual understanding on common ground especially related to the concept of Confucian Entrepreneurship. The analysis will base its roadmaps on the study of wisdom traditions generally, what they hold in common, and how they diverge on key points of interest likely to surface in BRI interactions.

Another largely unchartered area will describe how Christian missionaries both laypeople, nuns and priests have made a decisive contribution to China not only by sharing their values and beliefs but also in teaching hard sciences like mathematics, geography, and astronomy, to promote the development of a more objective understanding of China's complex relationship to the world beyond its borders. Invaluable lessons are drawn from this trial-and-error process of mutual education over centuries especially for successful negotiation and cooperation.

Leadership Training on International Business Ethics with a focus on Environmental Protection is based on various training seminars, series publications and conferences focused on "Respect for Nature in the Age of Environmental Responsibility and Carbon Reduction" organized by Rothlin Ltd. in China. The focus of this book is to report in concrete detail on what has been learned through these training seminars regarding green policy within the BRI as well as related to the implementation of the laws preventing water, soil and air pollution, in order to convey the challenges involved in promoting similar activities. The specific theme on environmental responsibility has been chosen, not only because of its intrinsic importance, but also because it well illustrates the problems involved in seeking to provide training on such a controversial topic.

"Corporate Philanthropy in China: A Handbook for Practitioners" is conceived as a sketch of the history of philanthropy in China, as well as an assessment of recent developments, beginning with responses to the catastrophic Wenchuan earthquake of 2008, culminating in the reforms of China's new Charity Law and its impact on the activities of firms doing business in China, both foreign and domestic. The handbook is meant for a non-specialist audience that is interested in exploring philanthropic activities consistent with doing business in China but seeks reliable background information on what to expect as it expands its operations there. This book also is a useful companion to several of the case studies featured in "Doing Good Business in China," which was published by World Scientific Press in 2021.

Stephan Rothlin
Macau
12 January 2022

About the Editors

Stephan Rothlin is the Director of the Macau Ricci Institute (www.riccimac.org). He serves also as the Founder and CEO of Rothlin International Management Consulting Ltd., located in Beijing and in Hong Kong (www.rothlin.org). His teaching and research interests are focused on international business ethics and responsible entrepreneurship with a focus on China. He provides educational consulting services to encourage the practice of corporate social responsibility, and advocates among business communities and society at large the values of honesty, integrity, respect, transparency, and responsibility as indispensable elements for excellence in business.

Dr. Rothlin completed his academic studies in 1991 with a Ph.D. in moral theology at the State University of Innsbruck, Austria, and is fluent in six languages, including Mandarin Chinese, English, Spanish, Italian, French, and German. From 1992 to 1998, he was the executive director of the Academic Centre, AKI, in Zürich and a research fellow at the Institute of Empirical Research in Economics of the University of Zürich in Switzerland. From 1998 to 2012, he served as a guest professor of international business ethics at The Beijing Center for Chinese Studies in Beijing. Since his relocation to Beijing in 1998, he has become a sought-after speaker on international business ethics, having taught at various business schools throughout Asia, including Renmin University, Peking

University, Tsinghua University, the Central Party School in Beijing, Hong Kong University, and INSEAD Business School, Singapore. From 2005 to 2013, he was secretary general for the Centre for International Business Ethics, Beijing, and chairman of the Association of International Business Ethics in Hong Kong.

His personal hobbies include playing classical piano and tennis.

Dennis P. McCann is the Research Director for the Rothlin International Management Consulting (Beijing). He was Professor Emeritus of Agnes Scott College, Atlanta/Decatur, Georgia, USA, from which he retired in 2011. McCann taught business ethics in the USA for over 30 years, and has been involved in research, lecturing, and teaching on business ethics in China and SE Asia for the past 20 years. He has been particularly concerned to identify culturally appropriate teaching materials for China and Asia, based on his ongoing research in the fields of philosophy and religious studies. McCann received his Ph.D. from the University of Chicago Divinity School in 1976, and his Licentiate in Sacred Theology (S.T.L.) from the Gregorian University in Rome, Italy, in 1972. In addition to his current focus on Asian business ethics, his fields of academic expertise include comparative religious ethics, philosophy of religion, Christian social ethics, and Catholic Social Teaching. The author of several books and dozens of scholarly articles, most recently he co-authored, with Stephan Rothlin, *International Business Ethics: Focus on China*, published by Springer-Verlag in 2015. Along with Prof. Lee Kam-hon and Ms. Mary Ann Ching Yuen, he published a book, *Christ and the Business Culture*, in 2012 (Chinese University Press in Hong Kong). Over the past 20 years, McCann has taught courses, given workshops, and lectured in universities in Hong Kong, China, Philippines, Malaysia, Japan, Thailand, Indonesia, East Timor, and India. Currently, as a Faculty Fellow at Silliman University, Dumaguete, Philippines, McCann teaches courses in the graduate school of the College of Liberal Arts and Sciences: "Ethics and Organizational Behavior", "Ethics and the Professions", and "Religion and Psychology".

Mike Thompson is adjunct professor at Gustavson School of Business, University of Victoria and cofounder and director of Impact Hub London. He is also a leader for Anthesis, the global sustainability consultancy and of GLO — Good Leaders Online, the global leadership selection, assessment, and development platform. He co-edited *Responsible Research for Better Business* with L. Zsolnai (Palgrave Macmillan, 2020).

About the Authors

Benoît Vermander is Professor of the School of Philosophy of Fudan University, Shanghai, where he teaches religious anthropology and the hermeneutics of Chinese Classics. He also heads the Xu-Ricci Dialogue Institute at Fudan. His publications include: *Corporate Social Responsibility in China* (World Scientific Press, 2014).

Sonny Shiu-Hing Lo is Professor and Deputy Director (Arts & Sciences) at HKU SPACE. His publications focus on the political history and development of Hong Kong and Macau, and cross-border crime, crime control and policing in Greater China.

Henri-Claude de Bettignies, Emeritus Professor of Asian Business, The Aviva Chair in Leadership and Responsibility, Emeritus, INSEAD, Fontainebleau, France & Singapore & Distinguished Emeritus Professor of Globally Responsible Leadership, China Europe International Business School (CEIBS), Shanghai. www.insead.edu, www.ceibs.edu

Roderick O'Brien is currently an Adjunct Research Fellow with the University of South Australia. Originally qualifying as a lawyer in Australia, his career has included the practice of law in industry, university teaching in Australia and China, and research. Along the way he has completed degrees in Asian Studies and Professional Ethics.

Johnny Hon is the Founder of Global Group International Holdings Ltd., an international business conglomerate with diverse interests ranging over banking, biotechnology, education, entertainment and leisure, financial services, financial technology, media, mining, property development and sports. Whilst building the Global Group of Companies, Dr. Hon has also managed to pursue a wide range of charitable, diplomatic and political interests.

Francis C. Nwachukwu is Researcher at the Library of the University of St. Joseph, Macau, with a focus on Information Management & Literacy, Market Research & Analytics, International Business & Entrepreneurship with a focus on Africa.

Helen Xu is currently employed in Reckitt China, an FMCG company, as Associate Regulatory Affairs Manager. Prior to that, she worked for Beijing Rothlin International Management Consulting Co., Ltd. as Project Manager and Research Coordinator from 2015 to 2018. With strong team collaboration and coworking with internal key stakeholders, she authored multiple case studies on code of conduct, business ethics, moral leadership, and corporate social responsibilities in China.

Helen holds dual Bachelor's degrees, in Applied Mathematics and Business Administration, from Beijing Institute of Technology.

Yang Hengda has been teaching at Renmin University of China since 1982 and won the "Excellent Teacher" Award from the Beijing Municipal Government. He is a professor of comparative culture emphasizing values, political philosophy and intellectual history, and supervises doctorate candidates in these fields. In the U.S., he has taught at Towson University and University of Massachusetts, and lectured at Dickinson College, Wheaton College. He has translated Nietzsche's complete works from German into Chinese.

Editorial Supervisory Team

Edmund Eh
University of St. Joseph, Macau

Claire Wang
University of International Business & Economics, Beijing

Jenny Lao-Philips
University of St. Joseph, Macau

Sonja Xia
University of St. Joseph, Macau

Dennis McCann
Silliman University, Dumaguete
Rothlin Ltd., Beijing & Hong Kong

Stephan Rothlin
Macau Ricci Institute
University of St. Joseph, Macau
Rothlin Ltd., Beijing & Hong Kong

Acknowledgment

The editors express their gratitude to the Macau Foundation, the Macau Ricci Institute and the University of Saint Joseph, Macau, for their generous support.

Contents

© 2022 World Scientific Publishing Company
https://doi.org/10.1142/9789811250231_0001

Chapter 1

What Does It Mean to Dialogue with China?

Dennis P. McCann

Philosophical clarifications of the general principles of dialogue, their presuppositions, and their expected benefits may sometimes be misleading. In fact, often cultural biases and hidden agendas render genuine dialogues impossible. Since we all have biases, these need to be accounted for, so that we can begin a dialogue on fresh terms, open to new discoveries, new possibilities for mutual understanding, and mutually beneficial collaboration.

But can we make a fresh start? The history of foreign relations with China seems not very promising. Imperial China, as we all learn, for centuries regarded itself as "The Middle Kingdom", more in a symbolic sense than as a literal, geographical identification. The Middle Kingdom, standing at the middle of the universe, the indispensable connection linking Humanity with Heaven and Earth, expected all other entities — all nations, states, tribes, and peoples — to recognize its claim to superiority. China's hegemony was to be recognized through the ritual of kowtowing to be performed by all ambassadors from abroad. Kowtowing to the Emperor was to be accompanied by tributary gifts acknowledging China's superiority. Dialogue was possible only on the basis of acknowledged submission.

An interesting and often overlooked chapter of genuine dialogue with China has been undertaken along different trade routes with missionaries of different beliefs: When Chinese monks set out to deepen their learning of Buddhist wisdom and sutras coming back and forth from India, it was not just a matter of exchange of religious ideas. Their amazing journeys were always closely related to significant insights into new scientific and technological advances. Later when Franciscans and Jesuits were embarking on the trade routes of the Silk Road, in China they are remembered not so much as believers of a foreign creed but as diplomats and professors of foreign sciences like mathematics, geography, geometry, cartography.

When Great Britain's Macartney mission of 1793, seeking to establish trading relations with China, refused to engage in the ritual of kowtowing, the stage was set for the next two centuries of intermittent warfare, mutual suspicion, the harboring of grievances that to this day undermine the prospects for dialogue with China. Lord Macartney's refusal to kowtow to the Emperor Qianlong resulted in the failure of his trade mission.[1] The Emperor issued a letter confirming the breakdown in negotiations, indicating that China had no need for trade with the West. The West responded with increasingly bitter rhetoric about Chinese arrogance, significantly reversing the openness to China and all things Chinese that had been in vogue throughout the 18th century, thanks to the glowing reports on Chinese civilization sent home by Jesuits and other foreign missionaries. As the 19th century wore on, mutual contempt and ignorance set the stage for the Opium Wars (1839–1842 and 1856–1860), and the "Unequal Treaties" by which China was forced to yield territory and major concessions to the foreign invaders. Under such circumstances, dialogue at best was a charade, trying to preserve some semblance of peace between China and its unwelcome guests. However, what is overlooked in frequent references to "Unequal Treaties" is the fact that from a wider historical perspective these clashes of different civilizations and attendant cultural misunderstandings paved the way for modern trade and contributed significantly to a growing connection between different regions which had so far been separated from each other.[2]

---

[1] See Alain Peyrefritte's book, The *Immobile Empire*, 1992, for a detailed presentation of the Macartney mission and its historic significance.

[2] Ray Huang's *China: A Macro History* (1997) provides deep insights into China's long-term developmental challenges, and how various events, including the 19th century travails and China's recovery a century later, all contribute to its contemporary rise and the prospects for dialogue today.

With the abdication and downfall of the last Qing Emperor, the Republican Era began with leaders like Dr Sun Yat-Sen who wanted to combine their experience of foreign cultures with their own Chinese culture. However, this was followed by a period of great political instability and civil war. The foundation of the People's Republic of China opened a period of marked distancing of China from foreign influence and an attack on all foreign religions culminating in the Cultural Revolution (1966–1976). It has gone down in modern history as the most devastating period in terms of destruction of cultures accompanied by an unprecedented breakdown of dialogue. New hope for dialogue with China was sparked by the open door policy introduced by Deng Xiaoping in 1978 and the promulgation of the PRC's State Constitution of 1982, which appeared to re-establish the rule of law and pave the way for China's economic integration into the global economy. China's formal entry into the WTO in 2001 inspired optimism in the West that China's political institutions would evolve toward genuine democracy, as the economy opened up to mutually beneficial trading relationships and cultural exchange. Later events, however, have cast a shadow over the prospects for dialogue, which only recently, with the implementation of the Belt and Road Initiative (BRI), have once again revived, along with an awareness of the challenges that stand in the way of progress.

China's Belt and Road Initiative (BRI) began in 2013. Ostensibly, the BRI (一带一路) is an effort by the PRC government to create a new international economic order, by securing a number of strategic partnerships with countries of the West ("Silk Road Economic Belt") and the south ("21st Century Maritime Silk Road") through infrastructure investments that will create roads, seaports, airports, railroads, railroad tunnels, dams, and communications facilities to benefit the development of China's partners. By January 2021, 140 countries and 31 international organizations had signed 205 BRI-related cooperation agreements with China.[3] The BRI is planned such that its goals would be achieved by 2049, to coincide with the centenary of the Maoist Revolution.

Needless to say, the ostensible benevolence of the BRI has generated a lot of controversy, and not just among China's strategic competitors in

---

[3]For an overview of the PRC government's official statements about the BRI, see the website of the State Council of the Peoples Republic of China devoted to it: http://english. www.gov.cn/beltAndRoad/. The current statistics for participation in the BRI are taken from the Belt and Road Portal 2021: https://www.yidaiyilu.gov.cn/xwzx/roll/77298.htm.

the West. What it may mean for dialogue with China needs to be reviewed. Dialogue, everyone hopes, involves a peaceable conversation, interactions intending to promote mutual understanding and genuine collaboration. But there is no absolute beginning for dialogue, as if dialogue can begin, or pretend to begin on a *tabula rasa*. Since there is always a context, whether we like it or not, dialogue requires self-discipline, which creates a willingness to listen, to set aside previous prejudices and seek fresh insights, while at the same time retaining a critical awareness of what has gone before, what worked, and what didn't in previous encounters between the parties involved. Dialogue requires honest self-reflection, patience, and a willingness to see things from the other's perspective, even if in the end one cannot fully embrace that perspective.

Foreigners who seek to dialogue with China must try to understand Chinese views of their own history. Granted, there is no single narrative of China's modern history that all Chinese will embrace; nevertheless, a "macro-historic" view (Huang, 1997) may be necessary to remind every-one of the immense complexity and "slow motion" consequences inherent in a historical approach which truly tries to grasp the core elements of China. A rich religious diversity is the legacy of that history, as is recognized in the PRC's Constitution of 1982, Article 36,[4] and subse-quent documents establishing the legality of Buddhism, Daoism, Islam, Protestantism, and Catholicism in China. These are organized and held accountable through legally registered organizations, the Buddhist Association of China, Chinese Taoist Association, Islamic Association of China, Three-Self Patriotic Movement, and Chinese Patriotic Catholic Association, all of which are regulated by the State Administration for Religious Affairs (SARA). Those seeking to engage in dialogue with China should be aware of China's religious history, and its continuing impact on any and all parties to that dialogue.

China's internal struggle over religions, spiritualities, and their impact on its cultural identity is especially important for interpreting what is unfolding under the banner of the BRI. After all, the Silk Road was the primary route that missionaries—Buddhist and Christian—and merchants—Muslim and Jewish—traveled, bringing their faiths with them to China, prior to the 16th century incursions of the "People from

---

[4]The official text of the PRC Constitution of 1982, as amended in 2004, is available at the website of the National People's Congress of the People's Republic of China: http://www.npc.gov.cn/zgrdw/englishnpc/Constitution/node_2825.htm.

the Great Western Ocean" bringing Catholicism as well as new opportunities for international trade and commerce. Interreligious dialogue with, in, and for China, therefore, needs to be considered as an important dimension of the BRI and similar policies. For the Silk Road, whether by land or by sea, remains a two-way thoroughfare, enabling Chinese peoples to expand their interactions with various cultures and civilizations that do not share the specifics—either the glories or the humiliations—of China's history. That history suggests that dialogue with China will not be simply a vehicle for expanding Chinese "soft power" or cultural influence. As in any dialogue, both parties expose themselves to challenges that will change the way they do things.

What are the lessons for dialogue with China that emerge from past experience? There are several clues about the way forward as well as its challenges:

- First of all, though dialogue rarely occurs in a vacuum in which cultural exchanges for the sake of mutual understanding can unfold, the achievement of mutual trust capable of sustaining transparency and accountability remains a possibility, however elusive. These are not only worthy goals, but also indispensable if peaceful coexistence among China and its competitors is to flourish.
- Second, adopting realistic expectations is incumbent upon all parties to the dialogue. It is unrealistic to postpone dialogue until each party acknowledges the equal dignity, as well as basic human rights, of all parties involved. Dialogue, of course, means entering into a relationship, but relationships among equals are the exception, rather than the rule; relationships will change over time, and changes are asymmetrical.
- Third, even if the relationships are asymmetrical, meaning that at any given moment one party is superior and the other subordinate, as in Confucius's understanding of the parent–child relationship, changes over time are likely to reverse the dynamics of dominance and dependency. The risk that asymmetrical relationships can become pathological, that is, creating forms of humiliating dependence and opportunities for exploitation, can only be mitigated if both parties are actually motivated by the benevolence (*Ren,* 仁) that enables them to trust one another in their interactions. If China's BRI dialogues are genuinely intended, in the spirit of Confucius, to promote reciprocity (*Shu,* 恕) then the development of the relationships must be guided by attitudes and practices demonstrating benevolence.

- Fourth, building trust through dialogue requires not only prior agreement on the goals to be pursued, but also a commitment to openness that can readily be verified by all parties to it. Trust is not something that can be formally declared, or enacted through a traditional banquet, and then presupposed without further ado. Building trust requires that the dialogue be ongoing, and that the terms of the collaboration be open to review and revision as needed. If one trusts one's partner, one will be flexible and accommodating, if and when either party requires it. Trust does not mean turning a blind eye to whatever is going on, nor failing to do due diligence. As US President Ronald Reagan memorably said, "Trust but verify" (Armstrong 2019).
- Fifth, friendship (*Péngyǒu*, 朋友) is and ought to be the goal of any genuine dialogue. But what is friendship? It cannot be reduced to relationships of convenience. It must be more than transactional, that is, a wary willingness to collaborate in the fulfillment of tasks at hand. Friendship develops over time, in response to changing circumstances, where the relationship becomes a bond—call it brotherhood or sisterhood—that transcends the circumstances in which it began. Dialogue with China challenges us to reflect on our experiences of friendship, how these began, how they developed, how they survived various crises. It requires both parties as their relationship unfolds to ask, "Who is China's true friend?" Is a friend one who parrots the party line whatever it happens to be, never offering any challenge or honest criticism? Or is a friend one who remains committed to the dialogue even when difficulties—misunderstandings, honest disagreements, unforeseen conflicts of interest, and other surprises—emerge? Is a true friend someone who agrees with you no matter what, or someone who is willing to confront you when you need to be challenged?

*

With these five general points in mind, we can examine the prospects for dialogue with China, by examining various perspectives on the BRI that have been featured in the essays published in the *Macau Ricci Institute Journal* (MRIJ). Instead of discouraging dialogue, these may help guide us toward success. The MRIJ, a bilingual journal published both in English and in Chinese characters, is focused on three core dimensions, namely: Comparative Spirituality, Moral Leadership, and Social Innovation. While these three dimensions are featured in each issue of the

MRIJ, the following essays have been selected for inclusion in this introductory volume, because of the series' focus on the BRI. As Stephan Rothlin argues in his editorial Preface, the challenge of achieving the BRI's stated goals requires us to embrace a "New Humanism" that will orient all parties toward mutual understanding and mutually beneficial collaboration. The BRI must not be reduced to a program for economic assistance through innovative infrastructure development, however important such material goals may be.

In remarks on the BRI given in April 2019, President Xi Jinping articulated a vision of "openness and inclusiveness" that could be transformative in the way participants live and work together to achieve their shared goals. The MRIJ discussions of the BRI are meant to respond to President Xi's vision, hoping to show what it would mean to put it fully into practice. Creating an international culture of "openness and inclusiveness", of course, is a tall order; nevertheless, as Rothlin points out, "The main ethical challenge for the partners in the BRI process seems to be whether they are willing to share basic common values such as dignity, honesty, truthfulness, reliability and integrity. In order to bring about a sustainable business model based on reciprocity and fairness, we at the Macau Ricci Institute believe the wisdom traditions of China have a decisive role to play".

*

We start, then, with Comparative Spirituality because it is clear that the path toward a New Humanism must stem from an appreciation of the common ground, morally and spiritually, shared by all BRI participants. Prof. Yang Hengda, from Renmin University in Beijing, starts us off with reflections on "The Spiritual Principles Indispensable for BRI Construction". Responding to President Xi's "dream of a 'community of shared interests, destiny and responsibility'", Yang shows how it resonates with the classic teachings of Confucianism. Arguing that "the realization of genuine 'community' is in the final analysis a spiritual issue, an issue of values", Yang suggests that a common orientation is possible by comparing Confucian teaching with the *Declaration toward a Global Ethic*, promulgated by the Parliament of the World's Religions in 1993. Confucian teaching identifies this community with the ideal *datong* (大同)—the commonwealth state, which affirms that "the world is like a home shared by all" (*The Book of Rites, Liji XI, Liyun* chapter).

The *datong* becomes a practical possibility when participants learn to practice two key characters, namely, *Zhong* (忠, "loyalty") and *Shu* (恕, "reciprocity"). The embodiment of these virtues in the practices of a *Junzi* (君子), the "exemplary person" or morally refined leader, can support "the foundation toward a global ethic, and the important spiritual principle of the community of shared interests, destiny and responsibility".

The diversity of religious traditions, not only in China, but also among her BRI partners, is reflected in the essays that follow Yang's development of Confucian teaching. Dennis McCann's essay, "Appreciating Islamic Business Ethics", provides a perspective on Islam, in the interests of promoting dialogue through increased commercial exchange. Religions have made their way along the Silk Road, along with traders and merchants. A basic understanding of Islamic ethics enables the development of business partnerships, for it provides a basis for mutual trust and accommodation. Neither Muslims nor Chinese are amoral in their ideas and norms for commercial practices. A bridge of ethical appreciation is not only possible, as the history of China shows, but is necessary for the development of western China, with its minority Muslim populations, but also for cooperative relationships with its neighbors. A similar point can be illustrated from Benoît Vermander's "Encountering Buddhism in Today's China. The Quest of Christian Cochini". Cochini's research and writings enable us to understand Buddhism's continuing impact in modern China, by tracing its transformation through the preservation of various shrines and temples, and the extraordinary achievements of eminent monks who have restored Buddhism's role in Chinese moral education. Buddhism deserves a seat at the table, so to speak, in any practical dialogue among China and its neighbors. Its traditions are not to be relegated to museums, for entertaining tourists, but must continue to show China and its partners a higher way to achieve peaceful reconciliation. Cochini attributes the success of Chinese Buddhism to the fact that Buddhism was conceived as a state-sponsored religion with full support of the State.

This section on Comparative Spirituality concludes with Dennis McCann's review of Antonio Spadaro's book *La Chiesa in Cina: Un Futuro da Scrivere* (*The Church in China: A Future yet to be Written*), which interprets the agreement signed by the Vatican and the PRC government in 2018 to establish common protocols for the appointment of Catholic bishops in China. While Catholicism is among the most venerable of China's religious traditions, the Church endured various waves of persecution after 1949, largely because of its perceived dependence on foreign missionaries and the legacy of Western colonialism. The PRC's attempts to "sinicize the Church", which means to make it obedient to the Communist Party, consistent with its approach to other religious associations controlled by the Party, led to the founding of the Patriotic Association of Catholics which appointed bishops, a right traditionally exercised by the Vatican. The 2018 agreement, however, is not just about Church leadership and international diplomacy. As the essays collected by Spadaro indicate, they are meant to enable the Church to restore normalcy to its ministries in China, so that Chinese Catholics can be reconciled with one another for the sake of increased harmony and stability in civil society as a whole. Here, too, the agreement indicates that Chinese Catholicism is not to be dismissed as a museum piece, but must be appreciated by all concerned as yet another source of spiritual guidance and comfort as China moves forward internationally. If the BRI projects are to succeed, all the religious and spiritual traditions of China and its partners should be mobilized to educate everyone to the benefits and proper practices of dialogue.

*

The second set of essays focuses on the challenge of Moral Leadership. The interreligious dialogues just considered suggest that there is an emerging spiritual and moral consensus readily translatable into ideals of moral leadership and the best practices they should support. Henri de Bettignies's essay, "Developing Responsible Leaders in China within a Global Context", observes that today's demands for moral leadership cannot be voiced exclusively to governments, but must find a response in business corporations if they are to be dealt with effectively. Dialogue with China is not a spectator sport, like professional tennis. Business leaders must participate in the dialogue, particularly since there is so little consensus regarding political systems and their capacities for transformative leadership. De Bettignies, who has closely observed developments in China and East Asia for more than thirty years, is well aware that business corporations have all-too-often failed the leadership test, especially when it comes to stewardship of our natural environment. His hope is that China, by living up to its professed vision of our future, will demonstrate new models of moral leadership, especially in the ways its schools train the coming generations for responsibility in both business and government. Mike Thompson's interview with Johnny Hon, "Doing Business with Moral Leadership and Faith", provides evidence to support the realism of de Bettingnies's hope. Johnny Hon is a prominent investor and entrepreneur who was awarded the Medal of Honor from the Hong Kong government for his dedicated community service. He attributes his success to the practice of his Christian faith, which enables him to approach the challenge of getting ahead and making money in a manner that enhances rather than diminishes his capacity for moral leadership. His story helps us understand how it is possible to do well while doing good.

The dialogue with China must include concrete examples of how moral leadership succeeds in creating a balance between achieving one's financial goals while continuing to grow spiritually and morally as a responsible citizen and fellow human being. Yang Hengda and Dennis McCann shift the focus back to the foundations for this model of moral leadership, in the Confucian classics. "The Ideal of *Junzi* Leadership for the Common Good" reconstructs Confucius's observations on the *Junzi* (君子), often translated as "the gentleman" or "exemplary moral person". But the *Junzi* should not be dismissed as an anachronism, a holdover from the Imperial Examination System that was terminated in 1911. Yang and McCann show that the *Junzi* is not only a relevant model of virtuous behavior for today, but also that it is or can be socially transformative. For the *Junzi* ideal to be effective, its relationship to the common good must be fully realized, and it must be reintroduced into Chinese moral education. Dialogue with China, therefore, must comprehend the challenge of restoring education for moral leadership, well integrated with the technical and entrepreneurial skills that dominate today's curriculum.

Roderick O'Brien's "Attributes of Moral Leadership: Eight Encounters along the Silk Road" concludes this section by presenting his findings on what moral leadership actually means in the minds of China's BRI partners. What are their expectations of moral leadership? O'Brien presents very concise answers: From Turkey, we hear a plea for "reciprocity"; from Hong Kong, "good governance"; from Kazakhstan, "transparency"; from Malaysia, "ethical credibility"; from Pakistan, "respect"; from China, "integrity"; from Switzerland, "humanity"; and from Singapore, "trust". Dialogue with China must have ample space for an exploration of the meaning of each of these terms, what they mean cross-culturally, why they are presented as defining the partners' expectations for the BRI projects. As O'Brien notes, this will not necessarily be an easy dialogue, since China's relations with each of these partners is "asymmetrical", insofar as

China is organizing and financing the projects, and thus has far greater power in each case than any of its partners. All the more reason for China to learn, from its own Confucian traditions, that moral leadership often requires acute listening skills, self-discipline, and thoughtful restraint.

*

The practical outcomes that may emerge from successful dialogue with China are illustrated in the third set of essays, on Social Innovation. The goal of the dialogue is mutual understanding, which is both an end in itself and an invitation to improved opportunities for collaboration. The first lesson to be learned from the BRI is that China is already well launched on the path toward social innovation. No longer can China's progress be dismissed as based simply on copying the innovations of others, as if the dialogue must be narrowly focused on protecting the intellectual property rights of its partners and competitors.

Helen Xu's case study, "Angel or Demon? The Ethics of Online Peer-to-Peer Lending", confronts us with the reality of Chinese technological development and the challenges raised by it. One of the obstacles to China's progress has been its relative lack of access to capital, capital to support a variety of projects, but in her case study, capital to fund education and personal development. China's entrepreneurs have begun using the internet to establish direct relationships between lenders and borrowers, thus enabling an empowering flow of capital to students and others in need of education and training. Online "Peer to Peer" lending schemes are a social innovation designed to address their needs. But how do they work? What, if anything, is to prevent them from becoming another instrument of exploitation, as borrowers fall prey to immoral and illegal demands from lenders? Here is an issue where dialogue is sorely needed, and yet it is mostly internal to Chinese people and their relationships with one another and their government. What can be learned from Helen Xu's case study of China's efforts to encourage, but also regulate, "Peer to Peer" lending schemes may provide a model allowing the spread of such online platforms among China's partners in the BRI.

Another promising indication of how dialogue may enhance social innovation is outlined in Sonny Lo Shiu-Hing's essay, "Police Cooperation and the Fight against Cross-Border Crime among the BRI Countries". Professor Lo is a political scientist, Deputy Director of Hong Kong University's School of Professional and Continuing Education, who has spent years monitoring the development of collaborative relationships among the People's Republic of China (PRC), Hong Kong, Macau, and Taiwan seeking to combat forms of telecommunications fraud that have multiplied with the commercial development of the internet. His study of these efforts demonstrates that successful dialogue among China and its BRI partners can enable social innovations like e-commerce to expand, while also creating a network of accountability to diminish the opportunities for predators seeking to use the internet to rip people off. Dialogue with China must be practical, if social innovations like the internet are to flourish and become a vehicle for fulfilling the goals—economic, political, social, and spiritual—that have inspired the BRI projects. If Hong Kong, Macau, and Taiwan can learn how to cooperate with China in developing fair and effective law enforcement against fraud, there is hope that similar dialogues among China's BRI partners can achieve similarly promising results.

Francis C. Nwachukwu, from the University of Macau's School of Business and Law, in an essay, "Is the Belt and Road Initiative in Africa Sustainable?", highlights the challenges that such dialogues must face, as China seeks to develop new forms of economic and social assistance in Africa. Nwachukwu notes the needs of African nations, particularly in the area of infrastructure projects, as well as the challenges, often resulting from "asymmetrical relationships". He offers the United Nations' Strategic Development Goals as guidelines for BRI collaboration. China's dialogue with Africa has the potential to move beyond the patterns of colonialist exploitation that have marred Africa's past relationships with its ostensible benefactors in the West. But that potential can only be realized if China carefully monitors the social and economic impact of BRI projects, aligning them with sustainable development, deepening "mutual understanding through cross-cultural exchanges, ensure[ing] no corruption, ensure[ing] environmental protection and the enforcement of acceptable labor standards".

The final essay in this section comes from Mike Thompson, one of the founding Co-Editors of the MRIJ, "The BRI: Opportunities and Challenges". Professor Thompson offers not just a recapitulation of the opportunities for BRI success, already outlined by President Xi Jinping, but also defines five overall challenges that a BRI emerging from a genuine dialogue with China must address: (1) Managing peaceful relations with a rising power, (2) Managing financialization and anti-corruption, (3) Managing conflicting views of justice and cooperation, (4) Advancing local educational development, (5) Managing cross-cultural understanding, and (6) Managing cross-border data flows. Dialogue with China, as we have learned so far, must be practical. Thompson underscores that lesson, in each case, by showing how these challenges can and ought to be managed. They do not resolve themselves automatically or through the intervention of some *deus ex machina*. Here, too, it is obvious how social innovations—many of which emerge from China's own recent experience—demonstrate the need for dialogue, if the BRI is to become sustainable. The basic characteristics of any successful dialogue must be learned and relearned, in the details of negotiation seeking consensus about proper ways to move forward for the mutual benefit of all concerned.

*

In 1595, in the city of Nanchang, at the request of Prince Jian'an, Matteo Ricci—fondly remembered in China as *Lì Mǎdòu* (利玛窦)—wrote his first treatise in Chinese characters, the *Jiaoyou lun* (交友論), *On Friendship: One Hundred Maxims for a Chinese Prince.* (Ricci, 2009) This collection of aphorisms was presented as a summary of Western philosophical thinking, broadly inspired by Cicero's dialogue, *Laelius* (On Friendship, *De Amiticia*), but deriving from various figures honored in the *philosophia perennis* as it was understood during the European Renaissance. Careful analysis of these Chinese aphorisms, however, indicate that they owe as much to Confucian teaching (Hosne, 2014; Esquerra, 2015); and thus can provide an enduring benchmark as to what is possible in genuine dialogue with China. Ricci's first aphorism, "My friend is not an other, but half of myself, and thus a second me—I must therefore regard my friend as myself", (Ricci, 2009, p. 91) sets the agenda for the remaining ninety-nine. Ostensibly, based on an observation made in passing in Aristotle's *Nichomachaean Ethics*, the saying highlights the uniqueness of friendship among the five basic relationships (*Wulun*) that a person seeks to live by. Unlike the familial bonds characterized by filial piety (*Xiao*), friendship (*Péngyǒu*) is freely entered into, and is more likely to support equality as an important element in the ethic of reciprocity (*Shu*) (Ricci, 2009, p. 111).

Both Western and Confucian traditions emphasize friendship as a sine-qua-non for the cultivation of virtue. The ideal of the *Junzi,* as Ricci also observed, is unthinkable apart from the development of friendship.

Indeed, the contrasting antitype, the *Xiaoren*, is epitomized in several sayings that condemn flatterers and others who would instrumentalize the appearance of friendship only for its immediate material advantages. As Ricci observes, "Whoever makes friends thinking only of personal profit without also considering the benefit of a friend is nothing more than a merchant, and cannot be called a friend". (Ricci, 2009, p. 103). Regarding the kind of dialogue that ought to characterize true friendship, Ricci has this to say: "Proper friends do not always agree with their friends, nor do they always disagree with their friends, but rather agree with them when they are reasonable and disagree with them when they are unreasonable. Direct speech is therefore the only responsibility of friendship" (Ricci, 2009, p. 97).

The collection of essays featured in this book are ultimately inspired by the vision of friendship articulated by Matteo Ricci and treasured by his Chinese admirers, even to this day. It may seem that conversations among Ming dynasty (1368–1644) Confucian literati and their fascinating foreign friends are too precious and antiquated to provide much guidance for practical dialogue with China today. But if we take the time to reflect, as our authors have done, we must admit that successful collaboration involving partners and competitors from diverse cultural and religious backgrounds does require friendship as the ultimate accomplishment of dialogue. This may seem like a lost art nowadays, but if so, we must rediscover it, if we are to move forward together. We hope that the essays we have selected for your inspection will confirm that demanding and rare dialogue with China, animating the prospects for a successful BRI, requires that all of us rediscover ways to become true friends, not only among ourselves, but also with one another.

References

Armstrong, F. (2019). "Trust but Verify". *Forbes* (October 21, 2019). Retrieved on June 20, 2021 from https://www.forbes.com/sites/frankarmstrong/2019/10/21/trust-but-verify/?sh=5675859b5873.

Belt and Road Portal (2021). Retrieved on June 20, 2021 from https://www.yidaiyilu.gov.cn/xwzx/roll/77298.htm.

Esquerra, P. (2015). "Pragmatic cultural accommodation: A study of Matteo Ricci's Chinese works". *ICU Comparative Culture. No. 47.* pp. 29–61. Retrieved on June 16, 2021 from https://core.ac.uk/download/pdf/234720099.pdf.

Hosne, A. C. (2014). "Friendship among Literati. Matteo Ricci SJ (1552–1610) in Late Ming China". *The Journal of Transcultural Studies*, 5(1). Retrieved on June 16, 2021, from https://heiup.uni-heidelberg.de/journals/index.php/transcultural/article/view/11362/8996.

Huang, R. (1997). *China: A Macro History*. New York: M. E. Sharpe.

National People's Congress of the People's Republic of China, "The Constitution of the People's Republic of China". Retrieved on June 20, 2021 from http://www.npc.gov.cn/zgrdw/englishnpc/Constitution/node_2825.htm.

Peyrefritte, A. (1992). *The Immobile Empire*. New York: Alfred A. Knopf.

Ricci, M. (2009). *On Friendship: One Hundred Maxims for a Chinese Prince* (1595). Translated and edited by Timothy Billings. New York: Columbia University Press.

State Council of the Peoples Republic of China, "The Belt and Road Initiative". Retrieved on June 14, 2021, from http://english.www.gov.cn/beltAndRoad/.

Comparative Spirituality

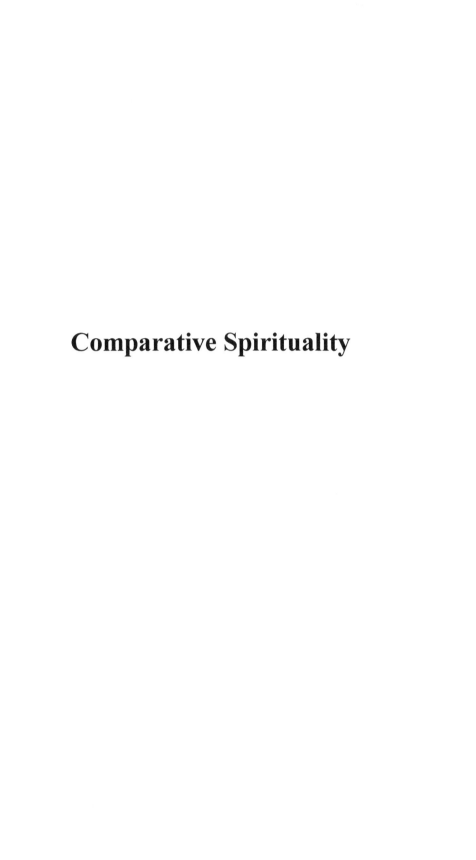

Chapter 2

The Spiritual Principles Indispensable for the BRI Construction*

Yang Hengda

Renmin University of China, Beijing, China

Abstract

The Belt and Road Initiative (BRI) proposed by China is now being carried out. The preparation for BRI is rich and sufficient. At the same time to achieve its material goals, the issue of values, ethics and spiritual principles is more and more attracting people's attention. President Xi advocates the spirit of the Silk Road and its intensive cultivation in the humanistic fields and cooperation among the humanities. His dream of a "community of shared interests, destiny and responsibility" will benefit mankind not only on the material side, but also on the spiritual side. The spiritual benefits especially will make the achievements of the BRI permanent. We therefore need to clarify the spiritual principles indispensable for the BRI construction, to help people all over the world to explore points of convergence with their own values, ethics, and spiritual beliefs, and invite them to unite in achieving the commonwealth state or grand harmony as advocated by Confucianism, that bears a family resemblance with the perspective advocated by the Parliament of World Religion's

---

*This chapter originally appeared in *Macau Ricci Institute Journal*, June 2019, Issue 4, pp. 88–97.

1993 *Declaration toward a Global Ethic*. Although the values are drawn from various cultural and political backgrounds that differ in thousands of ways, a common basic principle can, nevertheless, be found. That means there is always the possibility for people all over the world to find something common in their spiritual need. My paper will show that the wisdom of the Confucian "*Junzi*" ideal must play an important role in the formation of appropriate spiritual principles for BRI construction and the community of shared interests, destiny and responsibility.

The Spiritual Principles Indispensable for BRI Construction

The BRI Project initiated by the Chinese government is now under construction in an increasingly progressive and orderly way. As the BRI Progress, Contributions and Prospects report points out,

> The Belt and Road Initiative upholds the principles of extensive consultation, joint contribution, and shared benefits. It follows a Silk Road spirit featuring peace and cooperation, openness and inclusiveness, mutual learning and mutual benefit. It focuses on policy coordination, connectivity of infrastructure, unimpeded trade, financial integration, and closer people-to-people ties. It has turned ideas into actions and vision into reality, and the initiative itself into a public product widely welcomed by the international community (Office of the Leading Group for Promoting BRI, 2019).

This is the general principle animating the BRI's basic ideas and targets, intended to address the challenges along the BRI way, including different religions and faiths, different habits and customs, different political influences, different economic systems and levels, different cultures and cultivations, different values as well as different nations with unbalanced development. The problems inherited from previous history and the conflicts of realistic interests caused by differences in values and religious beliefs as well as by competition for resources such as petroleum, inevitably will create various difficulties for the BRI construction.

President Xi's "community of shared interests, destiny and responsibility" (hereinafter referred to as "community") is a great dream, and it involves not only capital investment, the building-up of a firm economic structure and an effective network of transportation, as well as cooperation based on a convergence of economic interests, but it also lies in the establishment of a spiritual principle universally applicable. The realization of genuine "community" is in the final analysis a spiritual issue, an issue of values, that is, it depends on whether a common orientation can be found in the basic values of different cultures. Five goals for the BRI were stated in the central Party journal *Qiushi* (Ou X., *et al.*, 2017, pp. 12–17). While four of these focused on the material and operational dimensions, the fifth goal emphasized closer people-to-people ties, following the direction asserted by President Xi Jinping, "to lay importance on the intensive cultivation in the humanistic fields, respect the different peoples' cultures and histories, customs and habits" (Xi, 2016). This fifth dimension, however, raises questions that require reflection on our common spiritual principles through the exchange and communication of values. We need to seek a basic principle that emerges from the common spiritual needs of people all over the world.

Although the values and ethical perspectives of all the religions in the world vary greatly, a promising way forward already may have been outlined for us in the *Declaration toward a Global Ethic*, passed by the initial Parliament of the World's Religions in 1993. The *Declaration* points out:

> We affirm that there is an irrevocable, unconditional norm for all areas of life, for families and communities, for races, nations and religions. There already exist ancient guidelines for human behaviour which are found in the teachings of the religions of the world and which are the condition for a sustainable world order (Parliament of the World's Religions, 1993, p. 2).

The set of shared core values is a spiritual principle, which transcends the materialistic concerns of life but at the same time is related closely to them. It is universally applicable to any societies, any individuals, any families, any races, any countries, and any religions, and expressed by different cultures in different forms.

We consider humankind our family. We must strive to be kind and generous. We must not live for ourselves alone, but should also serve others, never forgetting the children, the aged, the poor, the suffering, the disabled, the refugees, and the lonely. No person should ever be considered or treated as a second-class citizen or be exploited in any way whatsoever. There should be equal partnership between men and women. We must not commit any kind of sexual immorality. We must put behind us all forms of domination or abuse (Parliament of the World's Religions, 1993, p. 3).

Confucianism expressed a similar idea more than two thousand years ago:

> When the perfect order prevails, the world is like a home shared by all. Virtuous and worthy people are elected to public office, and capable persons hold posts of gainful employment in society; peace and trust among all people are the maxims of living. All people love and respect their own parents and children, as well as the parents and children of others. There is caring for the old; there are jobs for the adults; there are nourishment and education for the children. There is a means of support for the widows, and the widowers; for all who find themselves alone in the world; and for the disabled. Every man and woman has an appropriate role to play in the family and society. A sense of sharing displaces the effects of selfishness and materialism. A devotion to public duty leaves no room for idleness. Intrigues and conniving for ill gain are unknown. Villains such as thieves and robbers do not exist. The door to every home need never be locked and bolted by day or night. These are the characteristics of an ideal world, the commonwealth state (*Liji* IX, *Li-yun*).

The more practical implications of the Confucian ideal of "*datong*" (大同) — the great harmony or the commonwealth state, which affirms that "the world is like a home shared by all" — are as follows: (a) Every person should participate in its public affairs, and elect the leadership of ability, talent, and virtues, to build a harmonious society; (b) While every person cannot avoid taking his family as the starting point of his consideration of interests, at the same time he should take a broad view of the society, sharing the social responsibility of mutual caring, mutual assistance, and developing a harmonious society; (c) We must cooperate to develop the wealth and human force resources with sustainability; and

> The realization of genuine "community" is in the final analysis a spiritual issue, an issue of values, that is, it depends on whether a common orientation can be found in the basic values of different cultures.

(d) We must realize social security and harmony through integrity and mutual trust. This is not a utopian illusion, but the basic root of the spiritual guiding principles for achieving the BRI's "community of shared interests, destiny and responsibility" or of the "human destiny community".

But how can the "*datong's*" four points to be realized? There is a need to cultivate the personality of a "*Junzi*" (君子, "exemplary man", or as in James Legge's translation, "superior man") based on the two key characteristics "*Zhong*" (忠, "loyalty") and "*Shu*" (恕, "reciprocity") in Confucianism, because this is "one principle that can run through the whole of one's life" (*Confucian Analects*, 4.15). These can be counted as the two key concepts supporting the foundation toward a global ethic, and the important spiritual principle of the community of shared interests, destiny and responsibility.

"*Zhong*" (忠, loyalty) means faithfulness to one's own sincerity and cordialness, as well as one's own spiritual principle, that is, to recognize the world and the self with sincere mind and rectified heart, to treat other people with sincerity and cordialness by discarding the false and retaining the true. When Legge translated "为人谋而不忠乎" into "whether, in transacting business for others, I may have been not faithful" (*Confucian Analects*, 1.4), he understood "*Zhong* (忠)" clearly as faithfulness. If one is faithful to others and others' affairs, as well as to the truth of the world, one has to get rid of the disturbances caused by selfish interests and subjective prejudices. To understand "*Zhong*" in its right sense can help us to distinguish a true spiritual principle with universality from political strategy posed in a hypocritical way. Even if our goal is the "*datong*" (大同) or "human destiny community", according to Confucius, it is important to rectify the names (正名) — meaning to live by the truth in them — because "when names are not correct, what is said will not sound reasonable, affairs will not culminate in success" (*Confucian Analects*, 13.3).

From the perspective of moral understanding, a comparison of "shame" (*chi*) and "guilt" can establish the possibility of a consensus, a united front against the acts that violate the common basic spiritual principle.

"*Shu*" (恕, reciprocity)" is explained Confucius himself as "What you do not want done to yourself, do not do to others" (*Confucian Analects*, 15.24), which is a Chinese ethical creed as important as the Golden Rule in the West.

The two Chinese characters "*Zhong*" and "*Shu*" thus summarize the ethical foundation and moral ideal of the Chinese commitment to benevolence as the proper way to share interests, responsibility and destiny. This is the spiritual principle indispensable for the BRI construction.

"*Junzi*" held much in esteem by Confucianism is a model for carrying out this spiritual principle. "*Junzi*" is not innate. Mencius said, "Before Heaven lays a grand mission on a man, it will first distress him in the spirit and exhaust him in the body, causing him to suffer from hunger and poverty, and subverting every bit of his effort, with which to inspire his ambition, forge his endurance, and remedy his defects in capacity" (Mencius, 12.15). Those who can assume a grand mission must undergo the hard experience of toughening and self-cultivation. The self-cultivation of a "*Junzi*" is especially important. It helps to form a "*Junzi*'s" many excellent qualities. In contrast with "*xiaoren*" (小人, the mean man), the advantages of "*Junzi*'s" qualities stand out strikingly. For example, "The superior man (i.e. *Junzi*) is satisfied and composed; the mean man (i.e. *xiaoren*) is always full of distress" (*Confucian Analects*, 7.37). This means that "*Junzi*" knows satisfaction and has an open mind. "The superior man is catholic and not partisan. The mean man is partisan and not catholic" (*Confucian Analects*, 2.14). This means "*Junzi*" keeps friendly ties widely and never forms cliques with a few people. "The mind of the superior man is conversant with righteousness; the mind of the mean man is conversant with gain" (*Confucian Analects*, 4.16). This indicates that a "*Junzi*" understands well what righteousness means and knows how to deal with the relationship between righteousness and gain. "The superior man seeks to perfect the admirable qualities of men and does not seek to perfect their bad qualities. The mean man does the opposite of this" (*Confucian Analects*, 12.16). This means that a "*Junzi*" always helps others to realize their noble ideals but not their evil ideas. "The superior man is affable, but not adulatory; the mean man is adulatory, but not affable" (*Confucian Analects*, 13.23). This means that "*Junzi*" seeks harmony and mutual coordination, not superficial agreement with others. "What the superior man seeks, is in himself. What the mean man seeks, is in others" (*Confucian Analects*, 15.21). This means that a "*Junzi*" assumes but never escapes his own responsibility.

"Junzi" must be close to men who follow the *Dao* so as to learn from self-criticism and correct mistakes. In this way can he himself be a man who follows the *Dao*. Confucius says, "He who aims to be a man of complete virtue (i.e. *Junzi*), in his food does not seek to gratify his appetite, nor in his dwelling place does he seek the appliances of ease; he is earnest in what he is doing, and careful in his speech; he frequents the company of men of principle (i.e. men who follow the *Dao*) that he may be rectified: such a person may be said indeed to love to learn" (*Confucian Analects*, 1.14). *"Junzi"* do not think much of materialistic enjoyment and sensual satisfaction; on this point Confucius encourages us to learn from Yan Hui: "With a single bamboo dish of rice, a single gourd dish of drink, and living in his mean narrow lane, while others could not have endured the distress, he did not allow his joy to be affected by it" (*Confucian Analects*, 6.11). According to Confucius, *"Junzi"* pays more attention to action, that is, acts diligently, speaks carefully: "The superior man wishes to be slow in his speech and earnest in his conduct" (*Confucian Analects*, 4.24), or "He acts before he speaks, and afterwards speaks according to his actions" (*Confucian Analects*, 2.13). However, even if he does not speak, in his mind there is always a principle he follows in his action. So Confucius says: "The superior man bends his attention to what is radical. That being established, all practical courses naturally grow up".

Then what is the radical? How are we to understand its social implications? Confucius goes on: "Filial piety and fraternal submission — are they not the root of all benevolent actions?" (*Confucian Analects*, 1.2). According to the Confucian principle of *"Shu"* (恕, reciprocity, or, considering others in one's own place), this root is not confined within a family, but is widely social. Recall the words of Mencius: "Respect your own elders and extend such respect to those of others; cherish your own young and extend such cherishment to those of others" (*Mencius*, 1.7). Memorable and very typical is what Confucius says: "Wishing to be established himself, he seeks also to establish others; wishing to be enlarged himself, he seeks also to enlarge others" (*Confucian Analects*, 6.30). Therefore, from a cultivated root a lifelong principle emerges. This principle is evident in the guidance given by *"Junzi"* and saints as well as the spiritual representatives of different civilizations, which strengthen our capacities for carrying on exchange, communication and co-ordination. The *"Junzi"* does not strive for worldly recognition. If there should be contention, then it is a friendly competition, before which each is polite to the other, while during the process of competition, each is friendly to the other, focusing on win-win. After the competition, the rival friends will have a drink (*Confucian Analects*, 3.7).

The nature of the Confucian "*Junzi*" can be summarized as the four Chinese characters of "*li*" (礼, propriety), "*yi*" (义, righteousness), "*lian*" (廉, honesty), and "*chi*" (耻, shame) that are traditionally considered in China as the "four cardinal principles of the country". The first three characters have been involved in the above description of the "*Junzi*". Here the fourth characters "*chi*" should be clarified. The Chinese ethical culture is very different from the Western "guilt" culture. The Chinese may not know what guilt means in the Western culture, but like the Japanese (who have been influenced greatly by the Confucian culture), as described by Ruth Benedict, they hold that "*chi*" or shame is "the root of virtue. A man who is sensitive to it will carry out all the rules of good behaviour" (Benedict, p. 224). From the perspective of moral understanding, a comparison of "*chi*" and "guilt" can establish the possibility of a consensus, a united front against the acts that violate the common basic spiritual principle.

To go further into the spiritual wealth of ancient China, we find more ideas that relate to this spiritual principle. Mozi's "*jianai*" (兼爱, universal love), an idea that is often associated with Christian notions of fraternity, means "to treat the states of others as one's own, to regard the houses of others as one's own, and to treasure the bodies of others as one's own" (*Mozi*, Chapter 15); his "*feigong*" (非攻, the condemnation of war) forms part of the spiritual legacy of non-violence advocated by great men such as Jesus, Leo Tolstoy, Gandhi, and Martin Luther King; his idea of "*jieyong*" (节用, economizing expenditure) already anticipates modern thinking regarding the importance of practicing thrift in managing resources well so as to realize sustainable development, corresponding to the objectives upheld by the United Nations' Sustainable Development Goals (United Nations, 2019).

Conclusion

We need to reach a key common view that the universality of the spiritual principle indispensable for the "community" is above suspicion, because it originally exists in various cultures. But great efforts will have to be made to carry it out in mind and in action. Especially on the issue of the "community", not only is a shared spiritual principle needed, but we also need the ethical attitude and decision to carry out the principle perseveringly. In the final analysis, whether to take the initiative of the "community" as a political strategy or a spiritual principle with universality, it is the key to decide if the BRI can bring in the long run a sustainable benefit to the people along the zone of the BRI, even of the world.

References

Benedict, R. (1946). *The Chrysanthemum and the Sword*, Boston: Houghton Mifflin, 1st Mariner Books Edition, 2005.
Confucian Analects, Trans. Legge, J. Retrieved from https://wenku.baidu.com/view/7572bfd5ad51f01dc281f124.html.
Liji IX (Li-yun) Book of Rites. (2006). Chinese text project. Trans. Legge, J. Retrieved from http://ctext.org/liji/li-yun.
Mencius. (2015). *A New Annotated English Version*, Trans. Wu, G., Fuzhou, Fujian, China: Fujian Educational Press.
Mozi. (2006). Trans. Zhou, C. and Qi, R., Changsha, China: Hunan People's Publishing House.
Office of the Leading Group for Promoting BRI. (2019). BRI progress, contributions and prospects. Retrieved from http://en.sasac.gov.cn/2019/04/23/c_1327.html.
Ou, X., *et al.* (2017). The BRI: The centenary project to benefit all the mankind. *Qiushi*, No. 11.
Parliament of the World's Religions. (1993). *Declaration Toward a Global Ethic*. Retrieved from https://parliamentofreligions.org/pwr_resources/_includes/FCKcontent/File/TowardsAGlobalEthic.pdf.
United Nations. (2019). About the sustainable development goals. Retrieved from https://www.un.org/sustainabledevelopment/sustainable-development-goals/.
Xi, J. (April 29, 2016). Speech at the thirty-first collective study of the Politburo of the Central Party Committee.

Chapter 3

Appreciating Islamic Business Ethics*

Dennis P. McCann

Silliman University, Dumaguete, Philippines

Abstract

If the Belt and Road Initiative (BRI) is to achieve its goals, the Chinese people and their government must recognize the importance of their own diverse wisdom traditions, for establishing peaceful and mutually beneficial relationships with the peoples and countries that lie to the West along the Silk Road. Nowhere is this more apparent than in coming to appreciate Islamic Business Ethics. As one of the greatest of the world's religious communities, both in number of believers as well as in its influence, Islam is a faith tradition that has shaped business practices in the nations that adhere to it. This paper will explore Islamic faith and will map out what difference it makes in how Muslims think about business and market transactions. Related issues regarding the specific moral obligations all Muslims recognize as imperatives of justice and charity will be discussed, as well as the kinds of occupations that are forbidden (Haram) and permitted (Halal), marking the path of faithfulness. This paper is offered as an appreciative introduction to Islamic business ethics, with the intent of facilitating mutual trust not only in interreligious dialogue and collaboration, but also through a realization of the common

---

*This chapter originally appeared in *Macau Ricci Institute Journal*, June 2019, Issue 4, pp. 61–71.

ground upon which all wisdom traditions stand in their attempt to shape
and uphold good business practices.

If the Belt and Road Initiative (BRI) is to succeed even in its strategic
economic and political goals, those promoting it must come to grips with
the diverse cultures and religions that they will meet as they seek to do
business abroad. Many of these cultures have been shaped by Islamic faith
and practice, which is also a significant factor in the Chinese provinces west
of Xi'an.[1] A major question for Muslims is whether China can be trusted to
deal fairly with foreigners whose cultures differ significantly from China's
majority Han culture. Trust, of course, is a two-way street. If Chinese people
are to respect and seek to understand the ways of their non-Chinese partners,
the partners in turn must show themselves to be trustworthy. Building such
trust among diverse partners requires the expansion of transparency and
mutual accountability. The study of Islamic business ethics, not only in general, but also as it is interpreted in various Muslim countries, therefore ought
to be an important factor in building the trust that will be required for the
BRI to become a lasting success (Hamdan, 2017). In what follows, I will
outline the principles of Islamic business ethics, showing how they are
grounded in Islam's radical monotheism, and what practical consequences
they indicate for business transactions involving both Muslim and non-
Muslim business partners, clients and customers. My research suggests that
faith in Islam, focused on Muhammad's revelation of *Allah*'s will for
humanity as recorded in the *Qur'an*, and subsequent authoritative interpretations of it, is decisive for understanding not only the declared values
enshrined in Islamic business ethics, but also the seriousness with which
these are observed in Muslim business practices.[2] While this sketch must
remain focused on the principles of Islamic business ethics — which is

---

[1] Gerhard Böwering provides an impressive survey of the history of Islamic communities
in China and interprets their morality, showing its convergence and divergence from
Chinese moral philosophy in "Preliminary Observations on Islamic Ethics in the Chinese
Context" (Böwering, 2012).

[2] W. Travis Selmier II's essay, "The Belt and Road Initiative and the influence of Islamic
economies", is a useful introduction to the diversity of Islamic cultures, typically represented in the economies of Kazakhstan, Iran, and Pakistan. It suggests that what is presented here as introduction to basic principles is hardly sufficient for doing business with
Muslims, without local knowledge (Selmier, 2018).

conventionally located in the field of normative ethics — it cannot ignore a major and apparently universal problem — studied in the field of descriptive ethics — namely, the perceived discrepancy between declared Islamic values and actual practices among Muslim business people.[3] The discrepancy between "what ought to be" and "what actually happens" is no more acute in Islam than in any other perspective in religious ethics. All forms of religious ethics struggle with the problem and attempt to understand it and offer concrete proposals for overcoming it. Islam may have a different explanation accounting for how the problem arises for believers, but like the others it does offer concrete steps to realign one's conduct with one's declared values.

Islamic Faith as an Orientation to Good Business Ethics

Islamic ethics begins and ends with the Muslim's response of faith in *Allah*. But who or what is *Allah*?[4] *Allah* reveals Himself to us, in the *Qur'an*, as a personal God who is uniquely worthy of worship. Scholars have shown that Islam is but one version of Abrahamic religion, that is, the interrelated beliefs of Judaism, Christianity and Islam. *Allah* is one and the same as the God of Abraham, Moses' "I am who I am", as well as the One whom Jesus acknowledged as "Father". *Allah*'s existence and expectation for humanity are revealed through this line of prophets, the last and greatest of whom is Muhammad. In Islamic faith, the Great Ultimate is emphatically alive and passionately involved in this world, aware of all that we think, say and do, and responsive to our attempts to communicate with Him through prayer, worship, and the good that we do. What *Allah* demands of each person is given in the name, "Islam". Faith means total submission to the will of *Allah*, trusting in His justice and

---

[3]Contemporary Muslim literature on business ethics often addresses this universal discrepancy. One example is Safdar Alam's *Primer on Islamic Banking: An Introduction to Islamic Banking and Finance*, which not only explains how Islamic financial transactions work, but also provides a critical discussion of whether they actually do preserve faithfulness to Muslim moral and religious principles (Alam, 2019).
[4]Gerhard Böwering's essay, "Names and Images of God in the *Qur'an*", provides a basis for non-Muslims to understand how Islam's concept of *Allah* (God) is constructed from the passages of the *Qur'an*, thus showing how theology emerges from reflections on a Scripturally authoritative revelation (Böwering, 2010).

mercy, performing the deeds that are consistent with His will (*"halal"*) and avoiding those that are contrary to His will (*"haram"*). To live one's life in faithfulness to *Allah* is simply to live by the truth of human existence.

Islamic faithfulness has five touchstones or "Pillars of Islam" (*arkān al-Islām*) that define what this revelation means in practice. These five are the foundations of Muslim life:

- *Shahādah*: The profession of faith in the Oneness of God and the finality of the prophethood of Muhammad;
- *Salah*: Prescribed daily prayers, recited five times a day;
- *Zakat*: Concern for and almsgiving to the needy;
- *Sawm*: Self-purification through fasting, especially during the month of Ramadan; and
- *Hajj*: Pilgrimage to Mecca, at least once in one's lifetime, for those who are able (Zahid, n.d.; Schimmel, Mahdi and Rahman, 2019).

The most important of these is *Shahādah*, the confession of faith, the content of which is *Tawhīd*, meaning "unity" or belief in the Oneness of *Allah* or God. The centrality of *Tawhīd* is far more than conceptual, as if it were merely an abstract philosophical proposition. *Tawhīd* implies that all things are interrelated in God, that all thoughts, words, and deeds have deep ethical significance as signs of a Muslim's faith or lack thereof. The contrast term indicating a lack of faith is *shirk* (*širk*) or idolatry, suggesting the elevation of anyone or anything to a position of equality with *Allah*. *Allah* has no equals, *Allah* is totally, exclusively, and uniquely Absolute.[5] Idolatry in any form violates *Tawhīd*, for it fragments the unity of the world, introducing false principles or forces (idols) claiming powers over us that belong to God alone. Idolatry, therefore, is not simply a false religious practice, but a state of soul in which confusion reigns, where moral clarity becomes impossible because forces other than God become the basis of our survival and prosperity. Riches, or the love of money, for example, can easily become a manifestation of *shirk*, insofar

---

[5] *Cf.* Gerhard Böwering's essay, "God and his Attributes", in the *Encyclopaedia of the Qurān* (2018), for an in-depth treatment of these interrelated concepts.

as we place our trust in our savings accounts rather than relying on God's justice and mercy.

Each of the other Pillars also has profound meaning for Islamic business ethics. *Salah*, the ritual prayers said five times a day, ensures that faithful Muslims remain aware of the presence of *Allah* at all times. If they are faithful in performing *Salah* their minds will not stray from *Allah*'s will for them in every moment. *Zakat*, the practice of almsgiving or reserving a portion of one's wealth for charitable donations, reminds each believer that *Allah* alone has absolute ownership of the earth and any goods that a Muslim may have extracted from it. If *Allah* is the owner of all wealth,

Since *Allah* is the only absolute owner of anything, the creation of wealth through commerce must submit to *Allah*'s will as concretely and personally experienced in the actual vicissitudes, or uncertainties, of doing business.

then the use of that wealth must be directed by *Allah*'s express will for the world; in short, its uses must be consistent with the principles of justice and mercy, as revealed in the *Qu'ran* and the *hadith*. *Sawm*, or the rituals of fasting, reinforce the practical meaning of faith in *Allah*. Our bodies as well as our minds must be brought into submission (Islam) to the will of *Allah*. *Sawm* cultivates self-discipline which is essential to faithfulness. *Hajj*, the pilgrimage to Mecca, which should be on every Muslim's "bucket list", so to speak, offers a privileged opportunity to experience the meaning of *Tawhīd*, the unity of Muslims in a worldwide community of faith (*Ummah*).

The concrete guidance of Islam for business ethics, while rooted in the *Shahādah*, requires further explanation. A key distinction is between performing actions that are consistent with *Allah*'s will ("*halal*") and avoiding those that are contrary to his will ("*haram*") (Beekun, 1997, pp. 31–36). *Allah* alone can decree which acts are *halal* and which are *haram*. Though the difference is roughly equivalent to universally recognized ethical distinctions of right and wrong, good and bad, appropriate and inappropriate, in Islam the basis for the distinction is not human experience, or the wisdom of ancestral sages, or any codification of natural law or other paradigms of moral reasoning, but on the manifest will of *Allah* as revealed in the *Qur'an* and the *hadith*, authoritative teachings of His Prophet Muhammad.

The maxim, "Love *Allah* More Than Your Trade", should be a signal for others to be wise: you may encounter real limits to what people are willing to do to make more money.

Allah's instructions regarding *halal* and *haram* can be quite specific. Various occupations, for example, are praised or condemned using these terms. Contemporary treatises on Islamic business ethics identify the *halal* occupations as agriculture, and work in manufacturing industries, as well as various crafts and professions. "In general, then, Islam looks on work that fulfills a *halal* need in society as good, provided that the person performs it in an Islamic manner" (Beekun, 1997, p. 34). *Haram*, however, would be earnings from trading in alcohol and illegal drugs, representative of the prohibited category of *khamr*, highlighting their intoxicating and hallucinogenic effects (Beekun, 1997, p. 34), which are incompatible with the self-awareness achieved through faithfulness. Besides these two, "the manufacture of pictures, statues, etc., as objects of worship or as objects to be likened to *Allah*'s creations" is forbidden as *haram*, as is "the production and sale of *haram* goods", that is, goods used in committing sins, for example, pornography (Beekun, 1997, p. 35). Prostitution is also considered *haram*, and expressly condemned in the *hadith* (*Qur'an*, 24:33).[6] There is also the category of "*Al Garar* ... any kind of trade involving uncertainty, regarding an unspecified quantity to be exchanged or delivered. Futures trading is therefore prohibited in Islam. It involves the selling of commodities not yet in the possession of the seller...". (Beekun, 1997, p. 36). *Gharar*, in short, "occurs in all sorts of transactions where the subject matter, the price or the two, are not determined and fixed in advance. Speculative activities in capital markets, derivatives instruments and short-selling contracts are bright examples of *Gharar* in modern finance" (Uddin, 2015).

---

[6]The text cited by Beekun (*Qu'ran*, 24:33) explicitly condemns coerced sexual exploitation, that is, a situation in which one's "slave-girls" are forced to become prostitutes in order to make money for their masters.

The prohibition on futures trading, of course, invites more questions about the ethics of Islamic finance. The moral concern expressed in a variety of precepts — including the prohibition against usury, or money lending at any rate of interest — is that the uncertainties or risks involved in an investment scheme be shared equally. Islamic teaching, in the interest of both justice and mercy, insists that both the risks and the rewards be shared equally. Similarly, the prohibition of lending at interest, or *riba*, expresses a moral concern over the fact that the lender typically makes money without any fear of loss, while the debtor is saddled with all the risks involved in accepting a loan and paying it back. As Beekun observes, "There is no opportunity cost of lending money in Islam" (Beekun, 1997, p. 46), and thus no justice in paying interest to the lender in compensation for borrowing the lender's money. Furthermore, the prohibited practice of *riba* "simply increases the gap between the haves and the have nots" (*Ibid.*).

One may well ask, if *riba* is prohibited, how is Islamic finance possible?[7] How can commerce be *halal*, if *riba* is *haram*? Clearly, Islam encourages business development, but favors the creation of business partnerships, even those in which one partner supplies the capital or financing and the other partner supplies the labor and skills to enact their mutually agreed upon business plan. Such partnerships are *halal* (assuming all other aspects are *halal*, such as the kind of business they are doing together), so long as the parties "agree in advance how they will share any profits or loss. Should the venture capitalist be guaranteed a profit on his capital whether his partner makes a profit or a loss, it would be similar to usury" (Beekun, 1997, p. 48). Since *Allah* is the only absolute owner of anything, the creation of wealth through commerce must submit to *Allah*'s will as concretely and personally experienced in the actual vicissitudes, or uncertainties, of doing business. To try to limit one's exposure to the risks involved through schemes involving "*riba, gharar* and *maysir*" would be a form of idolatry (*shirk*), a usurpation of *Allah*'s own prerogative to bless or refrain from blessing our activities (Uddin, 2015).

As Beekun's *Islamic Business Ethics* makes clear, much of what is judged as *halal* coincides with universally recognized moral values in

[7]A well-reasoned, comprehensive and systematic answer to this question can be found in the work by Usman Hayat and Adeel Malik, *Islamic Finance: Ethics, Concepts, Practice* (2014).

business. Muslims are urged to accept the following principles, which resonate well with the teachings espoused by Christians, Jews, Buddhists, as well as Chinese entrepreneurs seeking to follow the ways of Confucius:

- "Be Honest and Truthful".
- "Keep Your Word".
- "Love *Allah* More Than Your Trade".
- "Deal with Muslims before Dealing with Non-Muslims".
- "Be Humble in how You Conduct Your Life".
- "Use Mutual Consultation in Your Affairs".
- "Do Not Deal in Fraud".
- "Do Not Bribe".
- "Deal Justly" (Beekun, 1997, pp. 64–67).

Each of these might well be accepted as common sense, except perhaps the fourth principle, "Deal with Muslims before Dealing with Non-Muslims". Why the preference for dealing with Muslims? If partnership is the preferred model of business development, the answer lies in the community of values assumed to support the partners in their mutual interactions. Dealing with fellow Muslims first recognizes the challenges involved in establishing trust among business partners. If the partners share the same faith, trust may be easier to achieve and sustain than if the partners have nothing in common other than their desire to make a profit.

The ultimate constraint, of course, is spiritual and beyond morality: "Love *Allah* More Than Your Trade". This is the love that emerges from Islamic faithfulness, which includes a proper fear or reverence for *Allah*, that would motivate Muslims to submit to *Allah*'s will rather than to seek to evade it through various schemes that implicitly devolve into idolatry (*shirk*). Love for *Allah* establishes moral limits to how business may and may not be conducted. To love *Allah* is to know His will as revealed in the *Qur'an* and the *hadith* — the revelations to the prophet Muhammad and the traditions based on them. Accepting these limits and abandoning any effort to evade or cheat on them, is — when understood in the light of faith — the only secure basis for prosperity, or even survival, in our lives.

This religious orientation to business ethics, nevertheless, can be applied to contemporary business practice, whose implications can be clarified using many of the conventional tools of international business ethics. Beekun, for example, organizes much of his presentation using the conventional categories of stakeholder theory, which allows him to highlight Islam's meaning for the various categories of persons typically involved in or affected by business activities. He quotes, for example, a code of ethics for Muslim businesses that organizes its pledges according to stakeholder groups: customers, suppliers and distributors, employees, competitors, stockholders, and the Islamic communities, which such businesses are expected to serve (Beekun, 1997, pp. 60–61).

Beekun also shows in detail how environmental responsibility (Beekun, 1997, pp. 53–54), corporate social responsibility (Beekun, 1997, pp. 55–57), and various commonly accepted management practices, such as appointing an ethics advocate within the firm (Beekun, 1997, p. 61) and performing a social audit (Beekun, 1997, pp. 63–64), are consistent with Islamic practice. Beekun demonstrates that Islamic business ethics is already an informed participant in the movement to promote international business ethics.

Islamic Business Ethics and the Challenges of the BRI

This brief sketch of Islamic business ethics suggests that interactions with Muslim business people can and should occur on the common moral ground inhabited by all people of good will. Where there are differences, these can be understood and accommodated, if both parties — Muslim and non-Muslim — are sincere in their desire to work together. Here are two examples, one negative, one positive:

Given the religious weight of the moral distinction between *halal* and *haram*, non-Muslims should never demand that Muslims participate in activities regarded as *haram*. Some traditional Chinese customs, such as banquets sealing a business deal, involving prodigious quantities of alcohol, or various pork dishes, or after-banquet visits to karaoke bars where prostitutes are available, are likely to be offensive and counterproductive, if offered to faithful Muslims. If you want to do business with faithful Muslims, you do not want to make them uncomfortable by involving them in compromising situations. The maxim, "Love *Allah* More Than Your Trade", should be a signal for others to be wise: you may encounter real limits to what people are willing to do to make more money.

The preference for forming partnerships with other Muslims suggests that non-Muslims would be wise to work through Muslim intermediaries when negotiating business with Muslim enterprises. Consulting with Muslims who have status within the *ummah*, who can advise non-Muslims on what is appropriate and inappropriate, may help expedite and simplify the process of learning how to work together productively for mutual benefit. Securing the conditions under which trust may develop is crucial to business success. If you are dealing with business people who identify themselves as Muslims, you should assume that Islam is central to their identity. To assume otherwise, unless there are clear indications to the contrary, may be regarded as an insult, a sign that you are not serious about doing business with them.

One of the great challenges of making BRI work is the opportunity to demonstrate that Chinese business people are capable of showing proper respect for the cultures of the people with whom they hope to do business. Many foreigners who have come to China have learned to appreciate — as did Matteo Ricci and his Jesuit companions — the universal significance of Confucian morality and its scholarly traditions. Through them, Europe first learned to appreciate Chinese culture, opening up the possibility of peaceful interactions in many areas, including commerce. BRI now provides Chinese entrepreneurs and trade representatives with an unprecedented opportunity to reciprocate. Learning to appreciate the principles of Islamic business ethics may be a major step forward demonstrating the inclusiveness of Chinese moral wisdom, supportive of China's effort to achieve a new standard of global benevolence.

References

Alam, S. (2019). *Primer on Islamic Banking: An Introduction to Islamic Banking and Finance*, Kindle Edition. Published online by Kindle Editions (2019) (http;/www.amazon.com/kindle ebooks).

Beekun, R. I. (1997). *Islamic Business Ethics*. Herndon, VA: International Institute of Islamic Thought. Published online by Kindle Editions, 2016.

Böwering, G. (2010). Names and Images of God in the *Qur'an*. In *I shraq: Yearbook of Islamic Philosophy, No. 1*. Moscow: Institute of Philosophy: Russian Academy of Sciences. pp. 268–283. Retrieved from https://iphras.ru/uplfile/smirnov/ishraq/1/bowering.pdf.

Böwering, G. (2012). Preliminary observations on Islamic ethics in the Chinese context. *Journal of International Business Ethics*, 5(2), 3–27. Retrieved from http://www.cibe.org.cn/uploadfile/otherfile/j52.pdf.

Böwering, G. (2018). God and his attributes. In *Encyclopaedia of the Qur'ān*, General Editor: Jane Dammen McAuliffe. Washington DC: Georgetown University. Retrieved from http://dx.doi.org.ezproxy.library.uvic.ca/10.1163/1875-3922_q3_EQCOM_00075.

Hayat, U. and Malik, A. (2014). *Islamic Finance: Ethics, Concepts, Practice.* Charlottesville, VA CFA Institute Research Foundation. Published online by Kindle Editions (2014) (http;/www.amazon.com/kindle ebooks) Kindle Edition.

Hamdan Bin Mohammed Smart University. (2017). News: Second China-UAE Conference on Islamic Banking & Finance explores international cooperation in support of 'One Belt, One Road' initiative. Retrieved from https://www.hbmsu.ac.ae/news/second-china-uae-conference-on-islamic-banking-finance-explores-international-cooperation.

Schimmel, A., Mahdi, M. S. and Rahman, F. (2019). Islam. *Encyclopaeda Britannica.* Retrieved from https://www.britannica.com/topic/Islam.

Selmier II, W. T. (2018). The Belt and Road Initiative and the influence of Islamic economies. *Economic and Political Studies*, 6(3), 257–277.

Uddin, M. A. (2015). Principles of Islamic finance: Prohibition of *Riba*, *Gharar* and *Maysir*. Kuala Lumpur, Malaysia: INCEIF. Retrieved from https://mpra.ub.uni-muenchen.de/67711/1/MPRA_paper_67711.pdf.

Zahid, I. (n.d.) Five pillars of Islam in *Islam 101*. Retrieved from http://www.islam101.com/dawah/pillars.html.

Chapter 4

Encountering Buddhism in Today's China — The Quest of Christian Cochini*

Benoît Vermander

Fudan University, Shanghai, China

Abstract

Christian Cochini (1929–2018), the author of *50 Great Masters of Chinese Buddhism*, was a man passionate about Chinese culture and Chinese religions, in particular. His love for China made him eager to foster intercultural and interreligious encounters. Before starting his Sinological studies he had specialized in the study of the Latin and Greek Fathers of the Church. His special attention paid to their monastic traditions certainly prepared the way later on for his encounter with Chinese Buddhism. After several years teaching in China, Taiwan, and Japan, he moved to Hong Kong and Macao, where he embarked on a program of study and encounter with Chinese Buddhism that kept him busy till the end of his life. From around 2000 onwards Cochini became a pilgrim, travelling to every major Buddhist temple in China, and to many lesser-known centers. He recorded their cultural and scriptural riches, and engaged in long conversations with elder Masters whom he loved and

---

*This chapter originally appeared in *Macau Ricci Institute Journal*, June 2019, Issue 4, pp. 51–60.

41

revered. Deeply anchored in the Catholic and Jesuit tradition himself, he believed that interreligious dialogue was a privileged way to appreciate the spiritual traditions of the whole of humankind, in the hope of opening up the minds and souls of people from every nation and culture. Cochini was a visionary, and, for him, interreligious encounter was key to the betterment of humankind. Cochini published two voluminous books that are the fruits of his countless pilgrimages. The first one is about Buddhist temples in China. The second one — which is the one reviewed here — is about eminent Buddhist Masters.

The Centrality of Buddhist Monastic Communities

D uring recent decades, China's religious awakening has manifested itself in many ways. One of its most notable expressions has been the rapid development of Buddhism, based on the reconstruction and expansion of the Buddhist monastic communities. This is not surprising; from the very beginning of Buddhist expansion in China, the monastic community has constituted the axis around which rotates the devotional practices, the beliefs and the institutional continuity of Buddhism. A liturgical place, the temple acts as a collective intercessor for the community of believers directing to it their wishes and their prayers, especially for the deceased. As places of learning, the great temples make it possible to carry on through several centuries the translation of the Buddhist canon into Chinese, one of the greatest editorial enterprises in history, and to multiply the interpretations of it. As a place of power, the temple knows how to negotiate its relationship with the political leaders of the locality and then of the Empire, although this model was held at bay at the time of the big persecution of the ninth century, partly due to the concentration of wealth realized by the monastic communities.

Erik Zürcher provides us with the best summary of the *modus operandi* proper to Chinese Buddhism:

> During the first three centuries of our era the dissemination of Buddhism in China was carried on at the popular level. In the 4th century, Buddhism starts reaching out to the elites, and the first large monasteries are established. Enriched by important donations, they keep developing by running social and economic activities: management of their estates, accumulation of capital, organisation of fairs and pawn shops, printing

press and guest houses. Chinese Buddhism has thus become a powerful religious power drawing its strength from this remarkable institution which is the monastery. But the amazing fact is that this great religious power came to pass without any form of central direction or coordination. Chinese Buddhism has always been an ocean of countless centers, big and small, of very different levels, the biggest ones sponsored by the Court and peopled with learned monks, the smallest ones vegetating in the villages and inhabited by some illiterate monks. In summary: a great institutional force, combined with a great weakness of organisation (Zürcher, 1990, pp. 26–27).

The reconstruction of Chinese Buddhism after the turmoil of the Cultural Revolution relied therefore on the monastic institution, as was already the case in other times. And the vitality of the monasteries bears witness to that of the Buddhist practices and beliefs in the whole of the society.

It is not so easy to describe the Chinese Buddhist world in its totality. Monks and nuns, be they still novices or already ordained, are as easily identified by their clothing, their tonsure, and, for those who have been ordained, by their ordination certificates as by the scars on the head following the fulfilled rites. But the faithful are not recognizable in the crowd of those who visit the temples, so great is the diversity of their motivations and behaviors. The term, "Buddhist faithful" (居士), is normally reserved for those who have formally taken refuge (皈依) in the "three Jewels": The Buddha, the Law, and the Community. In return they receive a certificate that they can show at the entrance of a temple to be exempted from paying admission fees, for instance, or to get board and lodging. The levels of membership are many and not always so clearly identified.

The visitor to a Buddhist monastery will generally be struck by the predominance of young monks, often already at the head of their monasteries, sometimes graduated from prestigious universities. These monks are more and more engrossed in their tasks — construction of buildings, setting up of research centers and libraries in social institutions. The production of these elites of clerics is facilitated by regulations reserving admission into Buddhist studies centers to those of less than thirty years of age on average. Besides these young monks, one will usually see some quite old and silent monks who had entered the monasteries at a very young age, and long before the turmoil of the sixties. Having already assimilated the spirit and traditions of the school to which their temple belonged, and managing to survive, even starting anew some communities at the beginning of the eighties, they had handed over their responsibilities to their successors.

Of course, with the passing of time, the absence of an intermediary generation, conspicuous between 1985 and 2000, is less visible now, and the generation in power today has progressively asserted its experience and its authority. The nature and the exercise of this authority depend mostly on a transformation in the economic bases of the monasteries. The exploitation of the agricultural estates was replaced by an increased dependence on donations (at first from overseas, then from local donors), on the help of government agencies (for the reconstruction of buildings in particular), on the practice of rituals, and on some specialized productions. The monks affiliated with a given monastery generally receive a modest allowance, in nature or in cash, in return for their liturgical talents or for other services. Some develop a congregation (and thus a revenue) of their own.

One cannot understand the present state of Chinese Buddhism by looking only at its two extremes — the time of its beginnings, when the basic shape of the monastic community has taken form, and the reconstruction boom of the last two or three decades. One must also say a word about the ups and downs of its history throughout the last 150 years, for the destructions of the Cultural Revolution had been preceded by those of the Taiping Rebellion (1851–1864), particularly in South China, a traditional Buddhist bastion. The subsequent effort of reconstruction coincided then with rising internal criticisms concerning the system of formation and the lack of respect towards monastic precepts. Seen in the Catholic perspective, Chinese Buddhism was entering the era of *aggiornamento*. Some of the reformer monks advocated mainly going back to the ancient disciplines, privileging a small number of select texts and practices of meditation. A little later, came another trend, of which the

> Neither the development of Chinese Buddhism today nor its social and cultural impact can be understood without resituating it within the more general context of the religious awakening of China.

monk Taixu (1890–1947) is the most well-known representative. This involved a modernization of Buddhism, following a method close to that of the Chinese Republicans of the beginning of the last century — the ideal of "science and democracy" applied, so to speak, to the religious sphere. The role of the laity was emphasized, and monastic education was similar in style to that of the western universities.

The creation, in the first half of the twentieth century, of the Chinese Buddhist Association, the popularization of a humanistic Buddhism or Buddhism in the world (人间佛教), the contact between monks and political leaders of that time — all these characteristics have helped shape the look of Chinese Buddhism after 1980. Nonetheless, the debates that characterized the revival of 1870–1940 continue today, as the Buddhist community seeks to define its relationship with a post-modern China in a state of constant transformation.

Neither the development of Chinese Buddhism today nor its social and cultural impact can be understood without resituating it within the more general context of the religious awakening of China. Of course, the question of the nature of the "religious" in China must be raised at once, and therefore the question of its awakening. In China, as it is commonly said, religion affects and is affected by everything surrounding it. Rites, pilgrimages, temples, congregations, and beliefs create a landscape where political, civilian and familial institutions are inextricably linked together in a whole, through which the community reproduces and

> Far from confining ourselves to an exotic world, the reading of this book enables us to enter a "global spiritual history" — marked by travels, exchanges, returns, long-term evolution.

regulates itself, and at the same time expresses a search for meaning and prosperity. It must also be emphasized that the very word "religion" (宗教) in the Chinese language is relatively new, a term borrowed from the Japanese language towards the end of the nineteenth century to express a reality which could not be found in the Chinese world. From this perspective, to speak of the "return of the religious" would be immediately questionable.

Nevertheless, China has experienced a progressive structuring of the religious sphere. When the scholars of the 1920s and 1930s affirmed that "China [did] not need religion", they acknowledged by the same token the distinction between the sphere of the religious and the other spheres of social activity, an evolution carried on through quite a few centuries.

In other words, Chinese religions are historical phenomena in perpetual evolution, redefinition and social specialization. Religions have developed with, against and beside the state; dogmas and norms of behavior have been asserted, questioned and developed. Having been stalled at the time of the Sino-Japanese war, the debate about the role of religious beliefs and institutions in individual and social life was revived after 1979.

Transmission Through Spiritual

Master Christian Cochini's first book, focused on temples, can be read as a kind of "composition of a place", as the notion is used in the *Spiritual Exercises* by Ignatius of Loyola: "Preamble I. This is the composition, seeing the place.... The 'composition' consists in seeing through the gaze of the imagination the material place where the object I want to contemplate is situated". Let us be quite clear about this: Cochini carried out a long and meticulous survey to compose his overview of those privileged places — the temples — which join together the monastic communities, the faithful and the historical evidence, which condense and perpetuate the living reality of Chinese Buddhism. If there was "imagination" in this regard, it was not anchored anywhere else than in the most scrupulous observation. However, and this is the meaning of the parallel I am suggesting, his *Guide to the Buddhist Temples* did construct some "spiritual places". These are the nodes and the junctions through which Buddhism makes its contribution to the Chinese social and cultural fabric as well as its contribution to the inner quest that all humanity pursues and shares throughout the ages. Cochini's perspective was not just concerned with buildings or monastic organization but above all with collective memory and what was at stake in such places. To construct the place is indeed to get ready to go from the visible world to the invisible stakes involved in it. By contrast, his new work, the *50 Great Masters of Chinese Buddhism*, calls to mind what Ignatius of Loyola asks from the person who starts a spiritual retreat once the place is composed: "It is to recall the narrative". What is told here are the stories for which these temples have often been the scene. Here are stories of men (more rarely women) who lived and worked in their own time and environment and were often incorporated into the unified historical narrative made official both by the state and by their religious tradition. These individual monks have also become collective types: they have become models on which Buddhist faithful, but also perhaps believers from other religions, evaluate and guide their own spiritual paths. Their influence is not limited to China. Quite a few monks studied in this book shaped the development of East Asian Buddhism as a whole — in Japan and Vietnam notably — and are considered the founders of Buddhist Schools in the whole of Asia.

Far from confining ourselves to an exotic world, the reading of this book enables us to enter a "global spiritual history" — marked by travels, exchanges, returns, long-term evolution. In that respect, the account of the life of Hui Neng (慧能), perhaps the best known of all the monks mentioned here, is a good example. At night, his abbot expelled him from the monastery, at the very moment when he confirmed the authenticity of Hui Neng's awakening however socially radical and religiously subversive it may have been. It seems that the purpose of the expulsion was to save Hui Neng's life, but can we not discern something else in the expulsion of the man who tells the inner truth? Somehow, his Master does not appear to be able to follow through to the end. The narrative has such force that it has left a mark on the imagination, so much so that it largely explains the success and astonishing fecundity of the Zen school in the Japanese world and nowadays also on a global scale. Here it appears difficult to separate a doctrine from the story of the life in which it was embodied. Hui Neng has become a type in the spiritual history of the world beyond schools and dogmas. A reading of Cochini's book will show that this type plays a part in guiding the lives and choices of monks who have come after him.

It is significant to note that while Chinese Buddhism has exerted (and still exercises) a spiritual influence that extends beyond its borders, it had first strongly, and at length, taken root in the heritage it was receiving — the ones of the first generations of monks coming, for the most part, from the Persian Empire. The first texts we possess are aimed at building up localized monastic communities — however, these texts are not reserved for the community of monks: many passages of the *Sutra in Forty-two Sections* (四十二章经) are clearly directed at all the faithful and define a middle way which makes asceticism and study a vocation shared by all. This is also the case with another text of the second century ascribed to Mouzi (牟子), whose *Settling of Doubts* (理惑论) is clearly aimed at an audience of Confucian scholars. That synthesis has been a characteristic of subsequent Chinese history, but even so it was not accomplished on the basis of a doctrinal weakening of the Buddhist tenets: between the third and seventh centuries, and under the impetus and the direction of some of the Masters whose biographies are in this book, the translation of the Buddhist Canon into Chinese established itself as the greatest enterprise of translation in history and deeply modified the evolution of the Chinese language itself. But that subject is beyond our scope here.

There is a final point to which I would like to draw the reader's attention: Cochini's book proves particularly useful for understanding the history and role of Buddhism in modern and contemporary China. The eminent place he has given to the Masters of the 20th century is a most fortunate choice. Chinese Buddhism experienced two transformations of the utmost importance in that century: the first one was a consequence of the destruction underwent during the Taiping rebellion as well as of the shock created by Westernization. Following the trauma of the Cultural Revolution, the second transformation took place from the middle of the 1980s onwards and relied on new political and social conditions to rebuild the monastic institutions and carry out an enterprise of religious education for all social classes, mainly in the cities. Therefore, the biographies of the last part of this volume acquire a special interest as we begin to appreciate the meaning and scope of the religious mutations unfolding throughout the second half of the last century.

But the book's importance in throwing light on the most contemporary period does not stop there: once again it is the long lineage of eminent monks, with spiritual connections formed between individuals who lived in different times, which provides models and inspiration for all people in the quest of a spiritual path. In other words, Buddhism today transforms China not only by the power of its institutions but even more by the impact of its long history, as it is taken on and reinterpreted by the monks and faithful who continue it. The biographies of monks form a chain, with some of its links recalled in this volume, and the chain looks likely to continue. Thanks are due to Christian Cochini for having helped us to locate Chinese Buddhism in a global spiritual history, which must continue to guide and inspire the whole of humankind.

Reference

Zürcher, E. (1990). *Bouddhisme, Christianisme et société chinoise*. Paris: Julliard.

https://doi.org/10.1142/9789811250231_0005

Chapter 5

Book Review: Antonio Spadaro S. J. (Ed.), 2019. *La Chiesa in Cina: Un Futuro da Scrivere* (Crocevia) (Italian Edition). Milano: Ancora Editrice.*

Dennis P. McCann

Research, Rothlin Ltd., Faculty Fellow, Silliman University, Dumaguete, Philippines

Abstract

La Chiesa in Cina features six essays by Jesuits involved in the company's mission in and for China, plus official texts of the agreement between the Vatican and the government of the People's Republic of China regarding the appointment of Catholic bishops in China, and Pope Francis's message to Chinese Catholics and the Universal Church explaining the agreement (22 September 2018). It also contains a Preface by the Vatican's Secretary of State, Cardinal Pietro Parolin, and Antonio Spadaro's editorial introduction. Given the expertise of the Jesuit contributors — Spadaro is editor of *La Civiltà Cattolica*, the prestigious and historic Jesuit review

---

*This chapter originally appeared in *Macau Ricci Institute Journal*, December 2019, Issue 5, pp. 107–117.

in Rome — and the official statements presented in this volume, it stands as the essential point of departure for any realistic analysis of what the Catholic Church hopes to accomplish with this agreement. The book is written in Italian, so one may hope that a Chinese and/or English translation of it may soon become available.

A Future Yet to Unfold

Everyone knows that the agreement between the governments of the People's Republic of China and the Roman Catholic Church is controversial. No sooner than it had been announced, it was also denounced as a "sellout to the communist government" (Sherwood, 2018). The result of years of diplomatic interactions spanning three Papacies (St. John Paul II and Benedict XVI, as well as Francis), the agreement was described by the Vatican as "the fruit of a gradual and reciprocal rapprochement", concerning "the nomination of bishops, a question of great importance for the life of the church", which "creates the conditions for greater collaboration" (Sherwood, 2018). In principle, the agreement resolves any lingering disputes over the legitimacy of Chinese Catholic bishops, whether previously approved by the Vatican or simply appointed by the Chinese Catholic Patriotic Association (CCPA). While the seven bishops who had not been previously reconciled with the Pope are all now admitted to full communion with the Roman Catholic Church, the reciprocity expected from the PRC government of recognizing the bishops that had been nominated by the Vatican has not yet occurred. Nevertheless, the Vatican and the PRC government have established procedures for collaborating on the future appointments of China's Catholic bishops, and jointly agreed to establish a new diocese at Chengde, in northeastern Hebei Province, the historic site of the Qing Emperors' summer residence.

The agreement on procedures for nominating and appointing Catholic bishops promises to be "of great importance for the life of the church", given that there are at least 40 episcopal vacancies to be filled in China (Harris, 2019). Nevertheless, the agreement comes at a time when the PRC government is pressuring all religious organizations toward strict conformity with its own political agenda. Why, then, would Pope Francis approve an agreement that institutionalizes the government's role in nominating Catholic bishops, apparently contrary to the declarations of Vatican II (1962–1965) and the 1983 revision of the Code of Canon Law (Mariani, 2018)? Answers to this question are evident in the book of essays edited by Antonio Spadaro, S.J., *La Chiesa in Cina: Un futuro da scrivere* (2019): As in so many of Pope Francis's initiatives, the emphasis must shift from the diplomatic, legal, and political issues all too prominent in the past, to the hope for creating space for new approaches to pastoral care and responsibility. If the Catholic Church is to develop naturally in China, it requires episcopal leadership, showing the way toward spiritual renewal through personal witness to Jesus Christ. As Pope Francis indicated, the agreement is not intended to restore a hierarchy of "bureaucrats" and "functionaries". The impression created by Spadaro and his colleagues is that the results of the agreement will be consistent with Pope Francis's approach to the church's renewal worldwide, as previously seen in his approach to global challenges like catastrophic climate change or internal questions like the priesthood ordination of married deacons in the Amazon basin of Brazil. What he hopes to achieve in China is no different than the message of *Evangelii gaudium,* his Apostolic Exhortation on "The Joy of the Gospel" (2013).

The essays collected in *La Chiesa in Cina: Un futuro da scrivere* (2019) provide not only authoritative accounts of the history of the negotiations leading to the September 22 Agreement, but also important perspectives on various aspects of the pastoral situation in China, that now may better be addressed in light of it. The collection begins with a Preface penned by the Vatican Secretary of State Pietro Cardinal Parolin. After acknowledging in detail Benedict XV's epoch-making encyclical, *Maximum Illud* (1919), which highlighted the church's aspirations to fulfill its mission of evangelization, independent of the burdensome legacy of European colonialisms, Parolin suggests how those aspirations may be fulfilled now in China through the processes of dialogue and reconciliation. If the church's attempt at a new pastoral approach is to be credible, a new attitude inspiring innovative practices is necessary. The context for understanding the significance of the September 22 Agreement is outlined by Antonio Spadaro, S.J. (Spadaro, 2019, pp. 13–32), who acknowledges the challenges that must be addressed, if the hope animating the Agreement is to be fulfilled. The challenges he sees are complex, because they overlap in various ways: spiritual, political, internal divisions, external pressures toward the "Sinicization" of religious institutions, and finally, the theological challenge. Underlying all of them is the challenge of building trust, which requires a long-term commitment, as well as patience, mutual respect, humility and honesty. The future yet to unfold can only be realized by moving beyond the zero-sum thinking that only counts winners and losers, while moving toward pastoral responses that demonstrate these qualities of hope.

Following Spadaro's overview, Federico Lombardi, S.J., provides a detailed review of "The History of the Relationship between China and the Holy See" (Spadaro, 2019, pp. 33–48). Beginning with the Opium Wars (1839–1842), and the establishment of a French protectorate over the Catholic churches in China, the recent history is marred by a series of shameful events, of colonial humiliations, sporadic persecutions, and revolutionary transformations, in which Chinese Catholicism came to be seen — particularly by the partisans who founded the People's Republic of China (PRC) — as a foreign religion, fundamentally hostile to Chinese governance and culture. While this is clearly a distorted picture of that history, it does describe the context in which recent Popes have attempted a reconciliation. Lombardi notes the change that occurred in the wake of Benedict XV's *Maximum Illud* (1919), and celebrates the memory of Cardinal Celso Constantini, the first apostolic delegate assigned to China, and his work paving the way for the consecration of the first ethnically Chinese bishops in 1926. Despite the disruptions of World War II and the civil war between the nationalists and the communists that followed, the church made progress among the Chinese people, only to fall afoul of the revolutionary government, especially when it turned its attention in 1950 to the reform of Chinese religious institutions, with the so-called "Three-Self Movement" — self-governing, self-maintaining, and self-developing — which led to the expulsion of all foreign missionaries, and the prohibition of all foreign financial support for Catholic institutions. The Bureau of Religious Affairs, which was to regulate all religious organizations and to align them with the policies of the PRC government, was founded in 1951. The Vatican responded by repeating its condemnations of communism and denouncing the so-called Patriotic Association among Catholics, as in Pius XII's encyclical letter, *Ad Sinarum Gentem* (1954). The CCPA's first unauthorized consecrations of Catholic bishops followed in 1958.

> If the Catholic Church is to develop naturally in China, it requires episcopal leadership, showing the way toward spiritual renewal through personal witness to Jesus Christ.

A thaw in the relationship was not to occur until after China repudiated the excesses of the Cultural Revolution (1966–1976). At that point, the long march toward reconciliation began with diplomatic initiatives supported by St. John Paul II, and the proclamation in 1982 of China's new Constitution which, among other things, recognized the legitimacy of five Chinese religions: Buddhism, Daoism, Islam, Protestantism and Catholicism. In subsequent years, the Catholic communities of China remained split between the "clandestine" and the "patriotic" churches, with considerable ambiguity and confusion in the relationship between the two. Lombardi rightly highlights the role of Aloysius Jin Luxian, S.J., the bishop of Shanghai, who, while at first lacking the formal appointment from the Vatican, nevertheless managed to train and ordain a generation of Chinese priests who served the needs of both communities. The history told by Lombardi makes clear that the ambiguous relationship had to be resolved, if Chinese Catholics were to realize the church's hope for full communion, and to contribute to China's development through the exercise of its authentic mission of evangelization. Understandably, Pope Francis and his advisers saw the urgent need to bring peace to the churches, even though the processes of reconciliation would require sacrifices on the part of many who had learned to survive in a limbo of near schism.

The remainder of the essays in this book, contributed by Benoît Vermander, S.J., Stephan Rothlin, S.J., Thierry Meynard, S.J., Joseph You

> The fact is that there is great vitality evident in the ways that Chinese Christians — both Catholic and Protestant — are renewing their own traditions to address the challenges of China's global awakening.

Guo Jiang, S.J., Antonio Spadaro, S.J., and Michel Chambon, illuminate various aspects of the pastoral challenge and opportunities that may be addressed, now that the Agreement has been signed. Each one of these makes an invaluable contribution, because they alert readers to what is going on, and how Catholics may respond with hope, wisdom, and courage, as China continues to transform itself in this epoch of unprecedented social and economic development.

Benoît Vermander's essay on Christianity becoming more Chinese should help correct the false impression that "Sinicization" is just a government plot to further weaken the influence of the churches (Spadaro, 2019, pp. 49–60). On the contrary, it is an opportunity for Chinese Catholicism to fulfill the vision of the earliest Jesuit missionaries, inspired by Matteo Ricci, S.J., who recognized that the opportunity for cultural synthesis in China was every bit as historic as the encounter between earliest Christianity and the Hellenistic culture of the Roman Empire. The future of the universal church yet to be written will depend, to a great extent, on how Chinese Catholicism develops, once the burdens of the past have been set aside. Vermander offers a second essay assessing the "religious and spiritual geography" of Shanghai (Spadaro, 2019, pp. 115–126), which highlights hopeful indications that at the level of ordinary people's experiences of religious community, that is, in their popular festivals and traditional practices, "the sacred" continues to flourish. What is left unsaid in his anthropologist's sampling of the soil of Shanghai's religious and spiritual life is how the struggle over control of the church's organizational structures may help or hinder the renewal of its mission of evangelization. No doubt the soil is amazingly fertile, given the history of Chinese attempts to suppress or co-opt Chinese religious and spiritual energies since the revolution, but the soil must be tilled, watered, and weeded, if there's to be an abundant harvest. In light of the September 22 Agreement the struggle is precisely over who will be allowed to do the tilling. On whose terms will "Sinicization" proceed, and with what goals in mind?

The challenge of urbanization is also developed in the essay presented by Antonio Spadaro and Michel Chambon on "urban Catholicism in China" (Spadaro, 2019, pp. 99–114), which provides an aerial view beyond what is happening in Shanghai. Patterns of internal migration, responding to China's dramatic development particularly in manufacturing for export, mean that the church's future cannot be focused on the rural villages where Catholic missions were once so successful. China is on the move, and mostly toward better economic opportunities in rapidly expanding urban areas. Effective strategies for pastoral care and evangelization must follow the people, as they and their religious needs respond to changing environments.

Similarly, the essay on "aggiornamento in Chinese Catholicism", presented by Thierry Meynard, S.J., and Michel Chambon, acknowledges the continued success of Chinese Protestantism in shaping Christianity in China (Spadaro, 2019, pp. 75–86). The growth rates for Protestant churches far surpass the relatively modest success of Catholicism. Rather than regard Chinese Protestantism as a rival, Meynard and Chambon ask what can be learned from it, so that Catholicism might similarly be renewed. They present an accurate sketch of Protestant development, beginning with the decision of many churches to work within the "Three-Self" Movement. While they also acknowledge all the historic vicissitudes that Chinese Protestants have faced — including the ongoing split between churches that are operating in conformity with government policy and those so-called "house churches" that are not — they admit that the clarity of Protestant evangelization focusing on faith in Jesus Christ as living Lord and personal Savior, along with the simplicity of their worship services and flexibility of church administration, is appealing to Chinese people. The lesson for Catholicism coincides with the spirit animating the September 22 Agreement: a genuinely pastoral approach that makes Catholic faith and practice equally transparent and accessible is the only way forward. As Chinese Catholicism continues to develop, ecumenical outreach with Chinese Protestants as well as interreligious dialogue with others must become a top priority.

What can be accomplished through such outreach is well illustrated in Joseph You Guo Jiang's, S.J., essay on NGOs ("Non-Governmental Organizations") in China (Spadaro, 2019, pp. 87–98). You's analysis of the situation facing NGOs reflects important recent changes in the government's laws regulating charitable activities. It is clear that the reform of these regulations was necessary in order to respond to the crisis in credibility that NGOs faced in the wake of highly publicized scandals following natural disasters like the 2008 Sichuan earthquake. The changes in government policy, therefore, should not be misread as an attempt to exclude religiously based charities and NGOs, but as a way toward greater accountability that will enable them to be more effective. Jiang's message is to encourage the continued development of Catholic NGOs in China, and in doing so he cites two case studies, both successful, the Protestant Amity Foundation and the Catholic Jinde Charities. Here, too, the path toward development must be pastorally motivated, consistent with Chinese law and regulations, and open to ecumenical collaboration.

The recent rise of NGOs, and concern over their activities, of course, is a reflection of the success of China's economic development. Chinese Protestantism has benefited dramatically from increased business activity, especially in the Pearl River Delta, where Christian entrepreneurs from Hong Kong and overseas are involved personally in the work of evangelization. Similar efforts are also underway among Chinese Catholics. Stephan Rothlin's experience in creating and distributing educational programs and materials to promote business ethics and corporate social responsibility is reflected in his essay on Catholic Social Teaching (CST) understood as a resource for business ethics (Spadaro, 2019, pp. 61–74). Rothlin emphasizes the importance of the Vatican's Justice and Peace Commission document on "The Vocation of the Business Leader" (2011), which is available in Chinese with the Shanghai Xu Guangqi Press (2015), as a basis for dialogue not only among Catholics but also with others facing the moral and spiritual challenges of today's business environment. The program outlined in that document — recalling the Catholic Action movement of a previous generation — "See-Judge-Act" — forms the basis for research and development of business ethics case studies available through the Rothlin Ltd. website (www.rothlin.org). Rothlin-sponsored research has also contributed to the development of an approach to business ethics, seeking to define a new cultural synthesis between CST and Confucian traditions of moral philosophy.

Taken together, the essays collected in Spadaro's *La Chiesa in Cina* (2019) show that the hope animating the Vatican's September 22 Agreement is not just wishful thinking. China is changing and there really are new opportunities for Catholic evangelization. Despite the discouraging impression created by a passing familiarity with the religious situation in China, namely, that the government is bent on eliminating all cultural and spiritual influences not directly under its own control, the fact is that there is great vitality evident in the ways that Chinese Christians — both Catholic and Protestant — are renewing their own traditions to address the challenges of China's global awakening. As these essays make clear, the Agreement is not an attempt to normalize institutional relationships, as if everything will then go on as it did before the Revolution of 1949, but should be received as a progress report on an open-ended process of reconciliation, not only between the Vatican and the PRC government, but also among the churches and the Chinese people. For Catholicism to develop properly, a pastorally oriented episcopal leadership is just as essential today as it has always been. The hope is that the Agreement will enable that leadership to emerge naturally among Chinese Catholics committed to serving the common good through witness to their Crucified and Risen Lord. One must also hope that this collection of essays will soon be translated into Chinese and English or both, so that the Church's stakeholders in China and abroad can also come to understand how and why there really is a future yet to be written.

References

Harris, E. (2019). Expert: New Chinese bishop no litmus test for success of Vatican-China deal. *Crux: Taking the Catholic Pulse*. Retrieved from https://cruxnow.com/church-in-asia/2019/08/28/expert-new-chinese-bishop-no-litmus-test-for-success-of-vatican-china-deal/.

Mariani, P. P. (2018). The extremely high stakes of the China-Vatican deal. *America: The Jesuit Review*. Retrieved from https://www.americamagazine.org/faith/2018/12/07/extremely-high-stakes-china-vatican-deal.

Sherwood, H. (2018). Vatican signs historic deal with China — but critics denounce sellout. *The Guardian*. Retrieved from https://www.theguardian.com/world/2018/sep/22/vatican-pope-francis-agreement-with-china-nominating-bishops.

Spadaro, A. (ed.) (2019). *La Chiesa in Cina: Un futuro da scrivere*. Milano: Ancora Editrice.

Moral Leadership

https://doi.org/10.1142/9789811250231_0006

Chapter 6

Developing Responsible Leaders in China Within a Global Context*

Henri-Claude de Bettignies

Henri-Claude de Bettignies is Aviva Chaired Emeritus Professor of Leadership and Responsibility, Emeritus Professor of Asian Business and Comparative Management, INSEAD, Distinguished Emeritus Professor of Globally Responsible Leadership, CEIBS, Shanghai, and Visiting Professor of International Business, Stanford University

Abstract

This chapter focuses on the influence of moral and responsible leaders on followers and corporations to lead change in their organizations. What is the nature of change and how can the moral dimension be heightened so that responsible leaders emerge to become a force for good in their societies and in the world? Given the failure of today's dominant economic model to deliver fairness, justice and happiness is there an opportunity for China to show a new way of harmonizing capitalism with a pursuit for the common good?

---

*This chapter originally appeared in *Macau Ricci Institute Journal*, September 2017, Issue 1, pp. 77–87.

Moral Leadership

Moral leadership is often seen as an oxymoron in societies where trust in political or business leaders is now very thin.

Moral leadership might also be seen as a tautology even though today leadership may not always be seen as being moral.

Leadership implies followership, a leader without followers is not a leader. Having followers implies that the leader has influence, is used to induce his/her follower(s) to behave in a certain way, and hence has a responsibility. Taking responsibility for others explicitly determines the moral dimension of leadership. This moral dimension is the essence of leadership and embedded in the nature of the leadership process, which is as it should be, and society expects it as do the leader's followers. But often it is not, as recent history recounts leaders who cut corners in terms of responsibility. They may end up in jail, sanctioned by society; they may lead their followers to disasters and they may take their organization to Chapter 11 bankruptcy protection. Their absence of moral leadership will, in any case, hurt others today or tomorrow.

> In managing change the leader's responsibility is critical. As a role model, the leader exemplifies values and so must "walk the talk" in order to nurture trust and build a shared vision.

Moral leadership is not an attribute of power expected only from an emperor with his "Mandate of Heaven", a king with his inherited power, a president elected by the citizens or a CEO appointed by a Board. Moral leadership is expected from anyone in a leadership position. The challenge is therefore to be a moral leader when circumstances or self-interest conflict with the values he/she holds or with the common good of the followers or of the society. Educational institutions are supposed to equip leaders or future leaders with the framework and the values that help to solve those unavoidable conflicts of interest or to handle the dilemmas encountered by leaders.

Leaders, in all walks of life, should see their contribution in making the future better as a categorical imperative embedded in the very nature of their position. Moral leadership thus becomes a prerequisite ingredient in any contemporary effort to further sustainable development. Today, in a world which is confronted by so many fast-changing and difficult issues moral leadership is indispensable to induce change but in a direction that will further the common good.

Leaders are change agents, driven by values. They propose a vision and a purpose, help to give meaning that should stimulate the followers' efforts to move them towards a goal that should drive their behavior. The challenge of developing and cultivating moral leadership is, initially, to contextualize the change taking place on our planet within which skills in managing change will be required by responsible leaders who are so much in demand today.

This is the first of two Viewpoint articles which aim to address two questions related to responsible leadership and change: "Will change in China make its future any better?" and "Are business schools able to contribute towards this process?" In this chapter I review change in the global context for responsible leadership with particular reference to China. In the next issue (not included here), I explore the question of whether and how business schools can groom responsible leaders who will contribute to the change journey underway in China.

Contextualizing Change: The Example of China

The performance of China over the last three decades arguably makes the country the best laboratory to observe change. Change is ubiquitous and has transformed China, its landscape, its cities and, to some extent, its people. In such a context the development of moral and responsible leaders becomes an imperative as change needs to be managed and influenced towards a desired outcome. Change needs leaders who propose a purpose which is conducive to the required skills.

Change is a broad, far-reaching topic that constantly recurs in management literature. It is of common concern among business leaders worldwide and in the mouth of politicians, a much-used buzzword. I first published a book on change as far back as 1971 (de Bettignies, 1971) in which I explore that the issue at stake is not change per se, but the management of change. Change is part of nature, highly visible, as we experience it. We experience it every day in some form or another. The real issue we need to address is how to manage change, how to leverage its benefits and control its costs and dysfunctions in order to ensure that it produces the desired ends.

This issue of change has absorbed me for many years. My first exploration into the subject took place in the early 1960s when I spent five years in Tokyo trying to understand how Japan was successfully resurrecting its economy by learning selectively from the West whilst carefully preserving its own distinct traditions and culture. More recently, again over five years between 2005 and 2011, I lived and worked in Shanghai to study China's transformation, its renaissance and re-emergence as the world's second global economy and its metamorphosis from a communist state to a wild capitalist environment, albeit with "Chinese characteristics". Today the speed of change in China over the last 30 years makes it the best environment in the world to study change. In between watching these two giants I was able to observe two other change cases at first hand. The first was Lee Kwan Yew's transformation of Singapore from a swamp into a thriving, rich "Switzerland of the East" and secondly, thanks to an invitation to spend every Spring term from 1988 onwards teaching at Stanford Graduate School of Business, Silicon Valley's ability over so many years to produce and maintain the spring of innovations that have changed our daily lives.

From these rich experiences I have learned some important lessons:

1. Change is not a decision, it is a process and has to be managed. Change takes time.
2. In managing change the leader's responsibility is critical. As a role model, the leader exemplifies values and so must "walk the talk" in order to nurture trust and build a shared vision.
3. Societal change implies change at the individual level. Change starts with "myself", i.e. my leadership behavior, my consumption patterns, and hence the critical importance of education.
4. The pace of change is accelerating and with it creating a sense of urgency that makes the introduction of the change process easier. Financialization, digitalization and globalization contribute to the increasing pace of change that results in the VUCA world of volatility, uncertainty, complexity and ambiguity.
5. To induce change at a country level, the development of solid institutions and the rule of law is a prerequisite. This task is particularly challenging for governments, which almost invariably lag behind technological evolution and its impact on society's expectations and on citizens' behavior.

Emerging economies like China, confronted by the many challenges stemming from this acceleration of change while trying to manage their own modernization process, have one advantage that was unavailable during the first industrial revolution in the late 19th century. They have a choice between several alternative models: a Western European model (with some diversity), a US model, a Soviet model or an original one, tailored to their particular history, culture and traditions. China, whose own "change journey" has resulted in the transformation of its economic, social institutions and practices and the building of a thriving society, is a good example of the effective management of change.

> How can a country become a modern nation whilst preserving its own values, traditions and culture?

For emerging economies such a journey is often long and the question of whether to look East towards China's amazing economic performance or West towards an increasingly dominant US model is an important one. How can a country become a modern nation whilst preserving its own values, traditions and culture? It is a delicate change process in our VUCA world where, on the one hand, we see how disruptive innovations such as "Uberization" can apparently create a crisis in a number of environments. On the other hand, as the case of China's president Xi Jinping seems to demonstrate, we observe the eradication of culturally inbred corruption which is not always a smooth process. China is able to leverage and develop its current assets: cheap operating costs, low wages, educated youth, the drive to succeed, the ambition to catch up and the so-visible tech-entrepreneurial drive that leads to multiple home-grown start-ups. But will these be the necessary and sufficient means to make China's future a better one in today's context? The Chinese are entangled in the globalization process and increasingly playing a part in the world community.

> Our predatory relationship with nature continues to exhaust primary resources, irreversibly pollute our natural environment and destroy biodiversity while we remain dangerously oblivious to the link between ecological transition and social justice.

Anyone in China, as in any other part of the world, who observes our environment can see how well-founded are current concerns about climate change, the consequences of the globalization process and the impact of digital technology. For we are now beginning to realize that the second industrial revolution that we are living through is unlike the first. It is not one that will displace some jobs whilst creating new occupations. Rather, as we go through one crisis (ecological, technological and financial) after another, it is becoming clear that we are being led into a new kind of civilization. Furthermore, we should be aware of the "elephant in this room"; for this new civilization is questioning our current model of living together and revealing the dominant model in the West and beyond as being obsolete.

Yesterday's map of the world is being re-drawn, with China quickly taking the lead and some of the BRICS countries and other emerging markets re-designing trade patterns.

Whilst Africa is maturing fast, an aging Europe continues to muddle through the challenging struggle to strengthen its identity and maintain its former influence. The US, for the time being, is still able to act as "Big Brother" or to play the role of "cop" in some parts of the world where there is conflict or turmoil, albeit at the price of dragging its friends into controversial wars.

Yet despite the growing challenges to its hegemony from China and Russia, the US remains the model for a number of emerging economies. People in China and the developing world still dream of an idealized American way of life even though the US pattern of consumption and waste means that it will remain an elusive objective and most likely remain just a dream. Despite this, both the US and Europe remain a magnet for many migrants trying to escape economic hardship or political hell, or who just hope to find an opportunity to nurture their talents. For the brightest brains in China, the attraction of exporting their skills abroad is obvious, even though their competencies are in great need at home.

Clearly, in China as in the West, we have not been the careful gardeners of the earth that we should have been. Our predatory relationship with nature continues to exhaust primary resources, irreversibly pollute our natural environment and destroy biodiversity while we remain dangerously oblivious to the link between ecological transition and social justice.

Representative democracy, which is "officially" the dominant model in 114 of the UN's 193 countries, requires the laborious construction of institutions, shared values and an acceptance of the rule of law, but today it elicits no admiration in China. Representative democracy is being widely questioned and, as its dysfunctions become more visible, is actually regressing in some countries. In politics generally, disillusioned citizens are skeptical of the short-term re-election objectives or populist behavior of their elected representatives. As money becomes the most important factor in the funding of election campaigns, confidence and trust in political systems is being diluted or completely shattered. The result is a democratic breakdown in which optimism that children will do better than their parents dwindles away, except in China. Rising income inequality becomes more visible[1] under the influence of wealthy elites shaping election outcomes via lobbying and funding campaigns.

> In politics generally, disillusioned citizens are skeptical of the short-term re-election objectives or populist behavior of their elected representatives.

"Capitalism and democracy", as the British business guru Charles Handy wrote, "make uneasy bedfellows" (Handy, 2015) and "capitalism with Chinese characteristics" is a clear illustration.

Although today's dominant economic model has significantly reduced the number of the poor living on our planet, it does not seem to have brought fairness, justice and happiness in its wake. Its growth objective, while apparently able to induce wealth creation, does not seem to be equally effective in bringing about wealth distribution. Highly visible and ever rising inequalities within and between countries lay bare the truth that wealth is not, as it was supposed to do, trickling down and that not every boat is being lifted on the rising tide. In a digital economy, the winner-takes-all model appears dominant as we watch Facebook buying Instagram and WhatsApp or Google dominating their markets and gobbling up any daring newcomers. If this picture is correct, and shared in China, then what hope is there for a better future? And who can be counted on to find a realistic, effective solution?

---

[1] In spite of the great improvement — from 35 percent of the world population living under the poverty level in 1993 to 14 percent in 2015 — today we still have 836 million who live with less than $1.25/day and according to WHO, 16.000 children still die every day.

Does Business Contribute to our Better Future?

To outside observers in the West, the recent behavior of the corporate world does not inspire optimism in its leaders. In the words of *The Economist*:

> "Confidence in business leaders is at a record low. An opinion poll by Edelman in 2014 showed that fewer than 50 percent of respondents trusted chief executives.... A recent review of the academic literature concluded that "one in every two leaders and managers" is judged to be ineffective (that is, a disappointment, incompetent, a mis-hire or a complete failure) in their current roles.... In 2011, nearly a sixth of the world's companies fired their CEO" (*The Economist*, 2015, p. 82).

As citizens in Europe and beyond see populists from both left and right rage against corporate greed, growing numbers of employees are becoming disengaged and absenteeism is on the increase. The corporate image has been tarnished by multiple scandals: Volkswagen, TEPCO, HSBC, Barclays, BNP Paribas, UBS to name a few. Scandals include environmental disasters directly attributable to company operations such as the BP oil spill, the Fukushima nuclear plant disaster and huge losses

> The trend towards filing profits overseas to avoid paying taxes in the home country further fuels the popular perception that large corporations are more concerned with value extraction than value creation.

of life due to the compromise of health and safety standards such as the Rana Plaza building collapse in Bangladesh and the employee suicides at Foxconn in China. Ethical scandals include corruption and money laundering, cartels and price fixing, insider trading and the rigging of foreign markets and have drastically undermined public trust in corporate leaders and crippled important stakeholder relationships.

Financiers have replaced engineers at the head of manufacturing companies so changing their culture, while the financialization of the economy has led to profit being put before people. Powerful, sophisticated algorithms and super-fast computers making possible high frequency trading have turned traders and their institutions into money-making machines, a trend seemingly followed by the whole corporate world.

China, today a world champion of high performance, is demonstrating its capacity to learn how to transform its economy effectively and to manage change, but let's be sure it is also moving towards a better future.

Extravagant executive compensation has increased wealth disparities.[2] As an FT editorial noted: "Few can see any justification, economic or moral, for the enormous widening gap between boardroom and workplace rewards, which is why the Occupy Wall Street movement and comparable protests around the world attracted such sympathy in 2011–2012" (Plender, 2015, p. 14).

Corporations buy their own stock to push up their share price and return on equity and then increase the component of their compensation packages linked to the share price[3]. The trend towards filing profits overseas to avoid paying taxes in the home country further fuels the popular perception that large corporations are more concerned with value extraction than value creation, and that they scorn the society that gives them the right to operate. In China responsibility for the Common Good often seems to have been outsourced to the moral leadership of the state.

The impact of corporate behavior on the environment, which it seems to view solely as a resource to be exploited, together with its definition of employees as just another resource to be used and/or abused further contributes to the widespread negative perception of the corporation. To manage these resources on a short-term basis and to deliver quarterly good news to shareholders within a highly competitive global environment put tremendous pressure on decision-makers to focus primarily on the bottom line. This in turn drives them to rely on lean manufacturing, cost cutting, head count and productivity gains, resulting in the disengagement of many employees. In large western corporations only 20 percent of employees

---

[2]Jenkins, P., writes: "...the best paid bosses in asset management such as Larry Fink of Black-Rock ($24m) are now on a par with the likes of J.P. Morgan's Jamie Dimon ($28m) or Goldman Sachs's Loyd Blankfein ($22m)". *Financial Times*, 20 October 2015 p. 14.

[3]Lazonick has demonstrated this in his study of the US situation from 2003 to 2012, showing that 90 percent of the large companies have invested 54 percent of their earning to buy back their own stock. Lazonick, W., Stock buybacks: from retain-and reinvest to downsize and distribute, Brookings Research Paper, 17 April 2015.

are said to be actively involved and committed to their firm. As a result, the bond between an individual and the organization now needs to be reconstructed. All these dysfunctions explain why, in some European countries, confidence in a growth ideology that would bring in its train so many negative externalities is eroding fast. Is such a trend also observable in China?

If we are to improve our future prospects, then we must accept that the "civilization change" challenges many of today's existing assumptions and that new technologies and changing values are bringing with them new problems for a new age. Digitalization and particularly social media may have given us more freedom and immense possibilities, but also demand greater responsibility for their use.

China, today a world champion of high performance, is demonstrating its capacity to learn how to transform its economy effectively and to manage change, but let's be sure it is also moving towards a better future. Such a future cannot merely be a cloning of a questionable western model. Rather, by leapfrogging Western countries China has the opportunity to learn from others' mistakes, to innovate and avoid the dominant model's shortcomings.

References

de Bettignies, H. C. (1971). *Maitriser le changement dans les organisations?* Paris: Editions d'Organisation.

Handy, C. (2015). *The Second Curve: Thoughts on Reinventing Society*. London: Random House.

Lazonick, W. (2015). Stock buybacks: From retain- and reinvest to downsize and distribute. Brookings Research Paper.

Petrella, R. (2015). *Au nom de l'Humanité*. Mons: Couleurs Livre.

Plender, J. (2015). *Capitalism: Money, Morals and Markets*. London: Biteback Publishing. *The Economist*. Leadership: Getting it Right.

Chapter 7

Doing Business with Moral Leadership and Faith*

Mike Thompson interviews Dr. Johnny Hon

Abstract

In each issue of *The MRI Journal* we feature an interview with a scholar, a business leader and other professionals who express their vocation and their expertise on one or more of the three platforms of the Journal: social innovation, moral leadership, and comparative spirituality. In this issue we report on our interview with Dr. Johnny Hon, a Hong Kong-based investor and businessman and leader of a range of business, charitable, diplomatic and political activities. In 1997, Dr. Hon founded the Global Group in Hong Kong which invests in business ventures all around the world helping innovative companies with their international expansion and financing strategies. Dr. Hon has helped numerous companies and individuals to raise funds and has been particularly active in assisting a growing number of Chinese companies to list on the London markets. In July 2015, he was awarded the Medal of Honour from the Government of Hong Kong for his dedicated community service.

---

*This chapter originally appeared in *Macau Ricci Institute Journal*, September 2018, Issue 2, pp. 80–86.

INTERVIEW Mike J. Thompson (MJT): Dr. Hon, what's your personal mission in life?

Johnny Hon (JH): My personal mission is to try to do good things, to try to help people, to make an impact and to develop things that are positive. I travel to different countries and work with different groups of people to help young companies develop. As a venture capital company we invest in start-ups and incubate them into big companies. We work as partners and as friends to try to make a positive impact in society.

MJT: What do you mean by positive impact?

JH: We try to change the world a little to make things better and, at the same time, we make good products good for consumers. I think everyone, big or small, can make positive contributions to the world.

MJT: How do you regard success?

JH: I think it's to have an interesting journey. You should be able to learn and become a better person while you are doing what you enjoy doing and doing it successfully. I measure success based on those points rather than just purely on financial gain. Based on my experience and the partners that we work with, people who are actually successful in business don't just do it for the money. They do it because they are passionate about what they want to do, to gain knowledge, to pass on the knowledge and to actually build something important. And I think that passion is actually the secret of success for a lot of entrepreneurs.

MJT: And how does that passion work itself out in the kind of projects that you would invest in?

JH: We love to invest in technology. We think that bringing technology to the developing world can help to change things. By working with a lot of smaller governments we try to help them develop the idea of entrepreneurship and innovation with IT and biotech-products and to build businesses that are sustainable.

MJT: How do you demonstrate care and respect in your business?

JH: Being in a venture capital business is actually the human capital business. What makes a business venture successful is the people around the business, so you have to do a lot of training, caring about people who work for you and learning from them. You create positive outcomes by growing together, the human side as well as the business side. Actually all my staff and partners have become friends.

Sometimes, when you face a problem or a difficult business decision, there has to be leadership. People have to take the lead to make decisions. But the big element of a successful business is communications with people who work for you, work with you, and you find common goals and achieve them together.

MJT: What are the challenges of business now from your perspective?

JH: Things certainly happen much faster and more short-term since the last few financial crises. One of the problems is that business leaders are very tempted to make short-term decisions and not to have a long-term aim. When I first started out, an investor expected a wait of 3 to 7 years to see returns. Now every 3 or 6 months you have to report returns and people give up on a deal so easily and so quickly. So, I think one does have to walk with the pace of the market and you do have to make fast decisions. Business leaders need to understand their own values and what they want to get out of a deal and stick to that. One of the hardest things is to try to be a good person and sometimes you pray to have the will and the power to be good given the fast changing world.

MJT: How does prayer help you?

JH: It gives you time to reorganise things in the fast changing world. When I pray the main theme is that I want God to give me the energy to be good. It's very easy to make mistakes and to go with short-termism. But every day is a new beginning and if you make mistakes, and the partners around you make mistakes, then forgiveness and understanding is a big part of it as well.

MJT: We can find it difficult to learn about forgiveness and to push back the ego. Our ego can get in the way of building quality relationships. What advice can you give our readers from your own experience?

JH: I think compassion, kindness, forgiveness and honesty are the important qualities for any business leader. When you work with people, you only want to work with people who, despite any mistakes, are underneath honest people with integrity.

MJT: How do we judge with practical wisdom? How do we judge when someone has got the values that you talk about?

> I think for a Christian doing business, making money shouldn't be the end goal, it's what you do with the money.

JH: I would say most people that we come across have those good qualities. It's just that in a world when things move so fast sometimes people get lost. But I think if they come to you, and if they know that you believe in something, it's very easy for them to be affected by you. As I said, I work with a lot of young entrepreneurs and young inventors and I try to help them with their business. They're looking for guidance, not just on the capital side. By working with them, you actually influence them and that is also how you make a positive impact.

MJT: Tell us what you are called to do in your business, Dr. Hon?

JH: I studied medical science and I was going to be a doctor. My PhD is in psychiatry and the reason why I made a big change to get into the business world was because I believed that if I became a successful businessman, I could influence things and help more people than I could do as a doctor. That's what I set out to do and that's always been my core value. So, I don't mind going into a difficult situation or difficult developing countries. I try to work with people who need assistance or business education or help. If you look at my career path, I've been to a lot of strange places. Making money is important because we need it to sustain things, but that is not the angle. The angle is to do good, that's my strong belief.

MJT: I guess that as you work with many of these companies and invest in different kinds of companies, you've been let down by people. How should a responsible business leader deal with such people?

JH: If you do a lot of business it's inevitable that you will meet people who will betray you, who will bad-mouth you and who will kind of grab what they can from you. At times, I have to admit that one gets very angry. But I think that forgiveness is important. One should also try to be more understanding, maybe to look at things from their point of view. You can get carried away with only thinking from your own perspective. I try to put myself in their shoes and try to find why. Maybe I've made mistakes myself and need to find some reasons behind all these actions. It's much easier for you to be able to forgive someone and realise that you yourself have made some mistakes and that you need to become a better person.

MJT: The Vocation of a Business Leader talks about the divided self, the part of me that wants to go for glory and be big, and then the other that wants to be more thoughtful and caring in life. The divided life can be the tension between my beliefs and my business life. Some people say business is business and we just have to be tough and I have to be two people. How would you respond to the idea of the divided self?

JH: As soon as you feel, "I'm good, I'm very good at what I do, I don't want to listen to others", then you stop learning. So, everyday what I try to say to myself is that I'm not good enough. I need to learn more and I need to become a better person. Having that attitude stops the ego from taking over what you want to do in your heart.

MJT: Dr. Hon, what does practical wisdom and making a good judgment really mean in practice in your professional life?

JH: When I look at business, I always look at the person behind it as a psychiatrist. My strong belief is that you need to look beyond the business plan and understand the entrepreneur. I actually believe that if an entrepreneur is a good person and he has good goals or values, then that is more important than the business plan. If you provide capital for young entrepreneurs it's very important to look at the person, not just the business plans. I normally leave my accountants to look at the figures and I just go and interview the principal myself.

MJT: You are motivated with a social purpose not just a business purpose. But many would say, "The business of business is business". How does social motivation fit in with doing business?

JH: I think if you look at the majority of successful business leaders in the world they have a philanthropic side to them. They would like to make money not just to keep the money but to try to do good with the money. I think that this is a fundamental secret for a business person to become successful because if you just focus on money you will miss out on so many things. By having the passion to do what you do, to enjoy what you do and to try to do good, you will get through the difficulties.

MJT: But here we are in Hong Kong, and there are many wealthy business people and there doesn't appear to be a lot of philanthropy.

JH: I think that if you talk to a lot of the billionaires, they've made money and there are signs that they want to help. Hong Kong, if you look at the figures, has the highest number of charitable donations in the world. There are a lot of charity functions being run here and people are trying to help. I think maybe you don't detect so much from looking from the outside, but actually there are so many charitable activities in Hong Kong and I think that's also one of the secrets of success.

MJT: What charities do you work with or support?

JH: I act as both the donor and fundraiser to help charities in the country to raise money from other individuals or corporations. I was chairman of 乐善堂 The Lok Sin Tong Benevolent Society Kowloon (LST) and helped to run things and to raise money. LST has about 1,000 staff, 18 schools and 4,000 volunteers.

MJT: So we may be confused in thinking that many business leaders aren't caring about society but, based on your experiences, many of them are caring about the world.

JH: Yes, certainly. When you look at Hong Kong as an example, it is a successful city on the whole. It has its problems like everywhere else, but when people talk about the core values of Hong Kong, they are basically Christian values. When kids go to school they are being taught that they need to be honest, they need to show kindness, they should do good. I think that this makes Hong Kong special because from those values, people will emphasize the rule of law and see the importance of justice. That's the fundamental reason why Hong Kong is so successful.

MJT: You talk about Christian values, so what is a distinctively Christian position on business?

JH: I think for a Christian doing business, making money shouldn't be the end goal, it's what you do with the money. I think it's a perfectly acceptable thing for any Christian to make money and then use that money for good causes and at the same time to try to pass experience on to and try to influence younger people or younger generations to do charity.

Dr. Johnny Hon is Chairman of Global Group International Holdings Ltd., Hong Kong.

Chapter 8

The Ideal of *Junzi* Leadership and Education for the Common Good*

Yang Hengda* and Dennis P. McCann†

Renmin University, Beijing, China

†*Silliman University, Philippines*

Abstract

The concept of the common good in both Western and Confucian phi-losophy presupposes a specific practical approach to moral education roughly identified as "virtue ethics". This paper will attempt to outline this approach as proposed in the Confucian classics, by focusing on the ideal of *Junzi* (君子) leadership — that is, the personal embodi-ment of moral excellence — and its relationship to the Grand Union (*Datong*, 大同), Confucius' symbol of the common good. Our focus will be on the practice of moral leadership — represented by the *Junzi* — describing how in Confucius' *Analects* (*Lunyu*, 論語) it unfolds in a process of self-cultivation whose goal is specified in the Golden Rule (*Analects* 15:24). Its outcome is a form of moral lead-ership capable of sustaining common good, inasmuch as the proper ordering of personal and social relationships becomes as natural as

---

*This chapter originally appeared in *Macau Ricci Institute Journal*, November 2018, Issue 3, pp. 15–25.

breathing. The concentric circles of responsibility, extending from personal to social — inclusive of care for family (*jiā*, 家), country (*guó*, 国), and the whole world (*tiān xià*, 天下) — provide a basis for envisioning an educational practice intending the common good. What takes root in the individual person naturally has social consequences.

The Junzi as Student and Teacher of Virtue

Can virtue be taught? Confucian ethics does not answer this question directly or in abstract philosophical terms. Its focus is practical, and therefore it demonstrates how virtue can be taught by actually teaching it. The *Analects* (*Lunyu*, 論語) is a collection of mostly aphorisms and a few extended narratives attributed to Confucius (551–479 BCE), China's universally acknowledged moral authority. The *Analects*, as well as the other Chinese classics attributed to Confucius, is meant to teach a Way of living that is consistent with human nature, the mandate of Heaven, and the testimony of one's venerable ancestors. Though the examples discussed in the *Analects* exhibit a specific concern for training Chinese elites in the art of governing well, Confucius makes clear that the Way forward is open to anyone who is willing to study hard and practice the art of self-cultivation. The *Analects* does not present a systematic summary of Confucius' teaching. Such a summary might actually be counterproductive pedagogically, since the point of Confucian study — which consists primarily of conversations with the Master among his students — is to learn from concrete examples of how and how not to behave, think and feel, consistent with becoming genuinely human. Education in the Confucian Way, therefore, is not about memorizing a series of basic principles and concepts. While Confucian tradition, like all moral traditions, has tended to prioritize the Master's sayings, as if his teaching could be captured in a single aphorism, or list of virtues, what these actually mean can only be learned through the practice of self-cultivation. The sayings presented in the *Analects* are to be savored, explored through meditation, through repeated attempts to reflect deeply on experience over a lifetime, the results of which should be shared with one's teacher and explored in common with his or her other students.

This much we can infer from the narratives of the *Analects*. Occasionally, however, the *Analects* offers a concise statement of principle that unlocks the meaning of the collected narratives. One such statement is the so-called Golden Rule, so readily used to summarize Confucius' teaching.

> Zi Gong asked, saying, 'Is there one word which may serve as a rule of practice for all one's life?' The Master said, 'Is not RECIPROCITY (*shu* 恕) such a word? What you do not want done to yourself, do not do to others.' (*Analects*, 15–24; *Kindle Locations*, 2847–2849).

Reciprocity is best understood by considering the parent-child relationship, and the ideal of filial piety (*xiào*, 孝). The parent nurtures the child for three years, and the child eventually mourns the parent for three years. Note, however, that reciprocity occurs within a relationship that unfolds over time; it cannot be experienced except in a relationship that is inevitably asymmetrical. At the end of three years nurturing at its mother's breast, a child is not expected to start supporting its parents. Over time it will learn what is expected by way of filial piety, and those expectations will change as the child eventually becomes responsible for its parents. Fulfilling the meaning of the "one word which may serve as a rule of practice for all one's life" will evolve as relationships change. What may not change is the common desire to be treated as a human being, and the common aversion to all things that detract from our humanity: "What you do not want done to yourself, do not do to others".

Even today, though the contexts of filial piety and reciprocity may have changed, the ideal of *Junzi* leadership is still informed by these constants. A leader following the *Junzi* ideal will start with a core assumption about his rivals, his employees, and all the stakeholders based on what he knows about himself. For example, since he does not expect hate from others, he should be inclined toward benevolence (*ren*, 仁) and righteousness (*yi*, 義) in his relations with others. A *Junzi* leader must love all people and be just and fair to them. The attitude to oneself and to others should be equally the same.

How one learns to live by the Golden Rule is not a spontaneous result of experience. The education of anyone becoming fully human must proceed through the study and practice of ritual propriety (*li*, 禮). The proper rituals communicate who we are — that is, the objective nature of the relationships in which we find ourselves — and what we must do to achieve

> The *Junzi*'s moral leadership is to be exercised in social organiza-
> tions, starting with the family, and expanding outward in his busi-
> ness or profession, whether for-profit or not-for-profit, whether in
> the agencies of government or social services.

harmony with Heaven, Earth, and Humanity as a whole. What is accomplished through such practices Confucian tradition remembers as "the
rectifications of names" (*zhèngmíng*, 正名). This is a hallmark of *Junzi*
leadership, insofar as good governance depends on calling things by their
proper names and acting accordingly.

> The duke Jing, of Qi, asked Confucius about government. Confucius
> replied, 'There is government, when the prince is prince, and the minis-
> ter is minister; when the father is father, and the son is son.' 'Good!' said
> the duke; 'if, indeed, the prince be not prince, the minister not minister,
> the father not father, and the son not son, although I have my revenue,
> can I enjoy it?' (*Analects*, 8:2; *Kindle Locations*, 2083–2087).

The rules of propriety (*li*) provide us with the proper understanding of
the roles and situations in which a person must act virtuously. To rectify
names, for example, the role of husband in relation to wife, or parent in
relation to child, one must correct one's way of thinking and acting by
narrowing the distance between one's actual practices and the ideal
expressed in the rules of propriety and their concrete realization in
the moral leadership of a *Junzi*. If the prince is truly a prince and therefore
known for his exemplary virtue, his ministers and the families they rule
will be virtuous as well.

Where to begin, then, in achieving the harmonious relationships that
Confucius thinks are possible? The answer is the ultimate in ritual propriety, namely, the practice of self-cultivation. How can a leader reach the
point of always keeping *Ren*, *Yi* and *Shu* in mind, and responding to others
through *li*? The ever-expanding virtuous circle depends upon universal-
izing the practice of self-cultivation "from the Son of Heaven down to the
mass of the people".

The *Analects* provides a number of insights into the practice of self-
cultivation. Achieving such a state of personal equilibrium or tranquility
requires more than study in the conventional sense. Apparently,

maintaining ritual propriety requires some form of meditation or personal reflection, beyond what is normally associated with acquiring knowledge through mastering facts and theories:

> Zi Lu asked what constituted the superior man. The Master said, 'The cultivation of himself in reverential carefulness.' 'And is this all?' said Zi Lu. 'He cultivates himself so as to give rest to others,' was the reply (*Analects*, 14:42; *Kindle Locations*, 2690–2693).

Reverential carefulness is a habit of mind, the fruit of the practice of self-cultivation, which enables persons to detach themselves from the ways of the world and its all-too-human striving for pleasure, recognition, and power over others. Without such detachment, any claim to moral leadership is spurious, as Confucius points out in the *Analects'* occasional comments on the attitudes of disciples who are not quite *Junzi* yet. The *Analects* does not describe in detail how the state of reverential carefulness is to be achieved; but its possession is clearly recognizable in the ways of the *Junzi*. Major clues for recognizing the *Junzi* are scattered throughout the *Analects* in the form of aphorisms contrasting the *Junzi* with small-minded people — or as Legge would have it, "the mean man" (*xiaoren*, 小人). Here are two memorable examples:

> The Master said, 'The superior man thinks of virtue; the small man thinks of comfort. The superior man thinks of the sanctions of law; the small man thinks of favours which he may receive.' (*Analects*, 4:11; (*Kindle Locations*, 538–543)

> The Master said, 'The mind of the superior man is conversant with righteousness; the mind of the mean man is conversant with gain.' (*Analects*, 4:16; (*Kindle Locations*, 569–571)

The Social Implications of *Junzi* Leadership

Although Confucius commends the *Junzi* as the embodiment of human benevolence and righteousness, this ideal is not an unattainable state of perfection symbolized in the legendary figure of the sage (*shengren*, 圣人). The *Junzi* is meant to convey a live option for all people who aspire to moral leadership. A leader must know very clearly his or her responsibility as a member of society, the moral equal of all other members of society. Confucius summarizes four of the characteristics of the *Junzi* — "in his conduct of himself, he was humble; in serving his superiors, he was respectful; in nourishing the people, he was kind; in ordering the people, he was just" (*Analects*, 5:16) — indicating that the virtues aspired to are inherently social. The *Junzi's* moral leadership is to be exercised in social organizations, starting with the family, and expanding outward in his business or profession, whether for-profit or not- for-profit, whether in the agencies of government or social services. The *Junzi* defines a moral ideal that transcends the institutional limits of the Warring States period in which Confucius lived, answering the question of how the common good is to be achieved in any social setting.

The Confucian classics contain a vision of the common good that could be realized were the *Junzi* ideal to animate the efforts of leadership in all walks of life. It is evident in the discussion of the Grand Union (*Datong*, 大同) presented in the Book of Rites (*Liji*, 礼记). When the Grand Union was observed, "a public and common spirit ruled all under the sky" in which all leaders strove for "harmony" based on "sincere words". Their spontaneous aspiration was toward a universal love, reminiscent of the teachings of Mozi:

> Thus men did not love their parents only, nor treat as children only their own sons. A competent provision was secured for the aged till their death, employment for the able-bodied, and the means of growing up to the young. They showed kindness and compassion to widows, orphans, childless men, and those who were disabled by disease, so that they were all sufficiently maintained (*Book of Rites*, 9 禮運; *Kindle Locations*, 5636–5639).

Full employment, apparently, was the aim of public policy, and all members of society contributed their labor toward the common good. "In this way (selfish) schemings were repressed and found no development. Robbers, filchers, and rebellious traitors did not show themselves, and hence the outer doors remained open, and were not shut" (*Book of Rites*, 9 禮運; *Kindle Locations*, 5641–5643). Confucian social philosophy starts with the assumption that working for the common good is natural, and that a society focused on the common good will expand naturally through its attraction for others. Thus "outer doors remained open, and were not shut". One can imagine how immigrants might be treated in such an open society. All are welcome who are willing to contribute to the common good.

But Confucius recognizes that the Grand Union is a legendary dream. While the *Datong* is not likely, what can be achieved is an approximation of the common good described as the Small Tranquility (*Xiaokang*, 小康). Unlike the Grand Union, the *Xiaokang* is characterized by an overriding loyalty to one's own family.

> Great men imagine it is the rule that their states should descend in their own families.... The rules of propriety and of what is right are regarded as the threads by which they seek to maintain in its correctness the relation between ruler and minister; in its generous regard that between father and son; in its harmony that between elder brother and younger; and in a community of sentiment that between husband and wife; and in accordance with them they frame buildings and measures; lay out the fields and hamlets (for the dwellings of the husbandmen); adjudge the superiority to men of valour and knowledge; and regulate their achievements with a view to their own advantage. Thus it is that (selfish) schemes and enterprises are constantly taking their rise, and recourse is had to arms; and thus it was (also) that Yu, Tang, Wen and Wu, king Cheng, and the duke of Zhou obtained their distinction (*Book of Rites*, 9 禮運; *Kindle Locations*, 5654–5663).

Clearly, the *Xiaokang* is not Confucius' ideal of the common good fully realized, but it may be as much of the common good as can be achieved in history as we know it. Instead of the spontaneous benevolence toward all people envisioned in the great Way (*Dadao*, 大道), everyone favors their own families. Even "the kingdom is a family inheritance". Given society's commitment to family as its organizing principle, achieving the common good consists in practicing filial piety (*xiào*, 孝), the rules of propriety establishing the proper norms for all social relationships. Moral leadership in a *Xiaokang* society, inspired by the example of the sage kings "Yu, Tang, Wen and Wu, king Cheng, and the duke of Zhou", is exercised by *Junzi* who observe the rules of propriety, providing good example whenever possible, and sufficient law enforcement whenever necessary:

> Of these six great men every one was very attentive to the rules of propriety, thus to secure the display of righteousness, the realisation of

sincerity, the exhibition of errors, the exemplification of benevolence, and the discussion of courtesy, showing the people all the normal virtues. Any rulers who did not follow this course were driven away by those who possessed power and position, and all regarded them as pests (*Book of Rites*, 9 禮運; *Kindle Locations*, 5663–5666).

> The challenge facing anyone who aspires to *Junzi* leadership is to live within a tension between the Grand Union — which may animate his or her deepest moral ideals — and the never finished business of maintaining and improving the Small Tranquility in which our lives unfold.

The common good achievable in a *Xiaokang* is a realistic possibility so long as those who aspire to become *Junzi* are properly educated. Confucius' destiny is to show how this might be done, through his words and his actions.

We have seen that the challenge facing anyone who aspires to *Junzi* leadership is to live within a tension between the Grand Union — which may animate his or her deepest moral ideals — and the never finished business of maintaining and improving the Small Tranquility in which our lives unfold. Of course, Confucius and his disciples knew that even the *Xiaokang* is but a hope for the best; if the morality defining the *Xiaokang* is ignored or perverted, an "Infirm State" (*Ci Guó*, 疵國) is the likely outcome, as society descends into "a state of darkness" characterized by war and poverty, while leaders become usurpers, bent on nothing higher than their own immediate advantage. Avoiding "the Infirm State" can happen only if society as a whole and its leaders embrace the morality embodied in the practices of the *Xiaokang*, which themselves imperfectly reflect the ideals of the *Dadao*. Understanding the *Junzi's* role in avoiding disaster and guiding everyone toward the harmony achievable in a Small Tranquility is central to any Confucian vision of education for the common good.

Junzi Leadership Intending the Common Good

What we all may yet learn from this Confucian perspective should include the following elements:

- First, the pursuit of the common good requires education, even more fundamentally than legislation or public policy reform.
- Second, education for the common good must reflect sound moral values, substantively embedded in wisdom traditions like the Confucian classics.
- Third, if it is to be pedagogically effective, education for the common good must focus on training in moral leadership. It cannot simply be a recital of general concepts reflecting moral ideals and aspirations, detached from a concern for the responsibilities of those who are capable of exercising leadership.
- Fourth, within such a focus on developing moral leadership, the emphasis must be practical, that is, it will investigate and propose the rules of propriety — or moral norms and virtues — that must be internalized by anyone claiming a leadership role.
- Fifth, this practical focus on cultivating a capacity for leadership must be grounded spiritually, that is, like the Confucian practice of self-cultivation which is central to *Junzi* leadership development, education for the common good will bear fruit or will wither on the vine depending on whether students master a technique of self-reflection or meditation that will create an habitual attitude of "reverential carefulness".
- Sixth, while making no claim to be a sage, the person trying to exercise moral leadership must seek to acquire virtues conducive toward inner harmony and personal tranquility, such as those that Confucius taught were characteristic of the *Junzi*: Humility, Filial Piety, Benevolence, and Righteousness (*Analects*, 5:16).
- Seventh, an authentic *Junzi* — that is, one who sincerely practices these virtues — will be recognized on account of them. A *Junzi*'s goodness will inspire goodness in others, who will naturally trust and cooperate with him or her in the pursuit of the common good.
- Eighth, the common good, if it is to be truly common, must emerge from the interaction of moral leaders with their followers, who will associate freely because of their mutual interest in achieving a truly common good.

In Confucius' own time — which is remembered as the close of the relatively peaceful Spring and Autumn period and the onslaught of the chaotic Warring States period — the ideal of the *Junzi* was proposed as a model for political leadership, for training rulers, ministers, and heads of families in their responsibilities for the common good. In our own day, in

China's period of economic and social reform, this same idea should challenge us as a model for leadership in business and the professions, the need for which is just as pressing as the need for a recovery of moral responsibility among all who would take up leadership roles. As we have indicated, *Junzi* leadership always demonstrates care for family (*jiā*, 家), country (*guó*, 国), and the whole world (*tiān xià*, 天下).

References

Confucius 孔子. *Great Learning.* Trans. Legge, J. Bilingual Edition, English and Chinese 大學: A Confucian Classic of Ancient Chinese Literature 四書. Lionshare Chinese Classics, 2016, Dragon Reader. Kindle Edition.

Confucius 孔子. *The Analects of Confucius.* Trans. Legge, J. Bilingual Edition, English and Chinese: 論語. Lionshare Chinese Classics, 2016, Dragon Reader. Kindle Edition.

Confucius 孔子. *Book of Rites, Liji.* Trans. Legge, J. Bilingual Edition, English and Chinese 禮記: Classic of Rites 禮經. Lionshare Chinese Classics. Lionshare Media, 2015. Kindle Edition.

https://doi.org/10.1142/9789811250231_0009

Chapter 9

Attributes of Moral Leadership: Eight Encounters Along the Silk Road*

Roderick O'Brien

Adjunct Research Fellow, University of South Australia

Abstract

The exercise of moral leadership within the Belt and Road Initiative (BRI) is not merely a theoretical study. Rather, the exercise of moral leadership is something that happens, and thus can be described. What would good moral leadership look like? This paper examines the writing of eight personalities along the BRI to identify some of the attributes of moral leadership. The attributes identified here are reciprocity, good governance, transparency, ethical credibility, respect, integrity, humanity, and trust. The eight personalities come from a variety of occupations, and from Asia and Europe. This survey is limited, yet it provides a useful beginning for wider examination.

---

*This chapter originally appeared in *Macau Ricci Institute Journal*, June 2019, Issue 4, pp. 29–39.

Introduction to the Belt and Road Initiative (BRI)

At the end of 2013 Chinese President Xi Jinping announced one of China's most ambitious foreign policy and economic initiatives. He called for the building of a Silk Road Economic Belt and a 21st Century Maritime Silk Road, now referred to as the Belt and Road Initiative (BRI). Analyst Peter Cai comments that BRI is arguably one of the largest development plans in modern history (Cai, 2017, p. 2). But BRI is not limited to infrastructure. It also encompasses cultural exchange and institutions, media, and educational projects (Xi, 2013) and (*Xinhua*, 2015a;b).

The approach of BRI is to create a series of bilateral relationships and projects. Nevertheless, the size of BRI has meant that there is already a need for multilateral structures, including the Asian International Investment Bank (AIIB).

A Chinese Initiative and a Multilateral Response

The BRI is an initiative by the Communist Party of China and the Chinese government. Most of the responses to this initiative comment on the Chinese position, but the attributes to which they refer should apply reciprocally. Thus if it is correct to call for transparency in China, then it is equally correct to call for transparency in Pakistan or Poland, in Singapore or Switzerland.

Also, while the BRI comprises a series of bilateral agreements, it takes on a multilateral dimension because of the need for co-operation by all the parties. The multilateral nature of the BRI may open up possibilities for renewed dialogue about universality. Some years ago, there was a debate about "Asian values". There were supporters for a variety of positions: that there could be Asian values which were not universal, or that there were no universal values, or that each polity decided its own values and their implementation. The multilateral nature of BRI will renew discussion about universality.

While the emphasis of this paper is on the testimonies of individual participants, we can begin with a context given in paragraph 14 of the Communique of Leaders at the conclusion of the Belt and Road Forum held in Beijing in 2017.

We uphold the spirit of peace, cooperation, openness, transparency, inclusiveness, equality, mutual learning, mutual benefit and mutual respect by strengthening cooperation on the basis of extensive consultation and the rule of law, joint efforts, shared benefits and equal opportunities for all. In this context we highlight the following principles guiding our cooperation, in accordance with our respective national laws and policies:

(a) Consultation on an equal footing…
(b) Mutual benefit…
(c) Harmony and inclusiveness…
(d) Market-based operation…
(e) Balance and sustainability… (*Communique*, 2017).

This paragraph suggests that values, principles, and attributes across the BRI are universal. However, the adoption or implementation of these values, principles, and attributes may prove to be contested, just as universal values have been contested in the past.

> If it is correct to call for transparency in China, then it is equally correct to call for transparency in Pakistan or Poland, in Singapore or Switzerland.

The participants featured here include academic researchers, a diplomat, journalists, a politician, and the leader of an international non-governmental organization. Their testimonies come from speeches at conferences, interviews with journalists, academic periodicals, and newspapers. Many of the sources cover a wide range of topics, but I have selected only one for each person.

Each brings their own experience to the encounter: Chinese author Xiao Yunru, for example, motored the old Silk Road from Chang'an (modern Xi'an) to Rome. He travelled 15,000 kilometers, and visited eight countries and thirty-one cities.

Attributes of Moral Leadership

The Oxford English Dictionary defines an attribute as "a quality or a feature regarded as a characteristic or inherent part of someone or something". This paper identifies attributes which can be regarded as characteristic or inherent for moral leaders who lead and implement the BRI. The method used was to search for a variety of responses to the BRI, using the Google search engine. Search words were "One Belt One Road", "Belt and Road", "ethics", "morality" and the names of countries…. Each response is an electronic "encounter" or meeting with the originator.

For the purpose of this chapter, eight commentators were selected from eight countries or organizations directly affected by the BRI. The commentators might be regarded as electronic "encounters" or meetings with the originator, each of whom expresses an attribute of moral leadership expected of the architects of BRI projects.

Abdulkadir Emin Önen (Turkey): Reciprocity

In November 2017, the Turkish newspaper *Daily Sabah* published an interview with Turkey's new Ambassador to China Abdulkadir Emin Önen (Önen, 2017). One of the topics was for Chinese and Turks to learn about each other's country and its culture. Ambassador Önen said:

> Our most significant handicap is that we learn Chinese culture from foreign sources.... There are many fields that the two countries share similarities, ranging from family structure to cultural life.

> In the short-term, our priority is to improve economic relations, trade and Chinese foreign direct investments in Turkey. We are also preparing many projects that will increase cooperation in culture and education which will bring to the countries closer [sic] (Önen, 2017).

Learning about each other and learning directly rather than through the mediation of foreign sources requires an attribute of reciprocity. BRI includes many nations, and if their relationships are truly reciprocal, then the sixty nations involved will each be enriched.

Ambassador Önen has referred to educational exchange. This is already taking place in at least one direction, as students from the Belt and Road countries find their way to China, and Chinese universities establish campuses abroad (Liu and Sukumaran, 2017). But this is only one step in the multiple reciprocities that facilitate introducing China to Turkey and vice versa.

Mimi Zou (Hong Kong): Good Governance

Professor Mimi Zou wrote as an academic from the Chinese University of Hong Kong, with expertise in labor law:

> A critical issue arises as to the ways in which the world's largest industrialising economy, in pursuing a new industrial development strategy

that will broaden its role in global markets and production networks in addition to its potential geopolitical influence, may shape the governance of international labour standards. Could China (including its public and private actors) become a new standard setter? Will Chinese firms drive a "race to the bottom" along the Belt and Road, especially in those countries with "weak governance zones"? (Zou, 2016).

Professor Zou identifies the International Labour Organisation as the key creator of international standards. Then, surveying the experience of Chinese workers at home and workers (both Chinese and local) employed by Chinese multi-national enterprises in other countries, Professor Zou provides examples of the low level of Chinese standards, especially in countries with "weak governance zones".

There is no doubt that China aspires to set standards. While China may achieve success in exporting its "hardware" technical standards, Professor Zou's work draws our attention to how China may shape standards in "software" fields such as labor relations. These standards may encourage good governance, or they may produce what Professor Zou has called "a race to the bottom".

Indeed, the sheer size and diversity of the BRI give it the potential to be a standard-setter in a wide variety of fields. Already there are new institutions such as the Asian International Investment Bank, providing an alternative to the existing financing structures. While the Asian International Investment Bank is a Chinese project, it has attracted significant international support and diverse interest.

Nargis Kassenova (Kazakhstan): Transparency

It was in Kazakhstan that Chinese leader Xi Jinping announced BRI, but there the details of BRI are only gradually being disclosed. Professor Nargis Kassenova of KIMEP University in Almaty, Kazakhstan, reviews some examples of the projects planned at the inter-governmental level, but also notes that the Kazakhstan government has yet to release the details of some projects already agreed upon with Chinese parties. She adds this comment:

If we want to benefit from the BRI projects, we need to approach it differently. One measure would be to increase transparency and inclusivity of decision-making. Basic information on projects should be available to the public. There is a need for public hearings in the parliament and consultation with the expert community (Kassenova, 2018).

Peter Chang Thiam Chai (Malaysia): Ethical Credibility

Dr. Chang of the University of Malaya writes in the context of Malaysia's recent change of government, and re-negotiation by incoming Prime Minister Mahathir Mohammad of deals made with China by former leader Najib Razak (Chang, 2018). He argues that some countries, including Malaysia, have reached a level of development of civil society in which giving exclusive priority to economic relations is no longer possible. Dr. Chang says that these societal changes require moral changes in China's way of dealing with Malaysia, and with other countries along the BRI. Dr. Chang writes:

> Moving forward, Beijing has to recalibrate its economic-centric approach with greater care for issues pertaining to civil liberties and restore its lost credibility with "cleaner" soft power…. Indeed, the People's Republic has enormous potential to positively affect the world. But Beijing must set in place stronger moral oversight…".

Dr. Chang concludes by linking moral leadership with China's own ancient ethical tradition:

> Apart from averting future ethical missteps, this enforcement will move modern China close in step with the much touted, idealized Confucian exemplary leadership, namely, "A ruler who governs virtuously is like the north star around which all other stars revolve".

Abdur Rehman Shah (Pakistan): Respect

Pakistan is a key country for the BRI, as this initiative now includes the China–Pakistan Economic Corridor (CPEC). Work on the Corridor is advancing and provides observers with early indications of how the whole initiative might take shape. Researcher Abdur Rehman Shah of the Centre for Research and Security Studies in Islamabad has written not only of the hopes for CPEC, but also of the limitations (Shah, 2018). For Shah, one of the potential areas of difficulty comes from the structural differences between the Chinese and Pakistani polities. Shah writes:

> As a democratically elected institution, the government of Pakistan is required to share the details of deals signed with the Chinese counterparts related to the CPEC in a transparent manner. However, the factor of transparency is clearly missing from this whole affair.

Incentives which favor Chinese stakeholders may be hidden in this opacity.

The structural differences in polities between Pakistan and China are not the only issue for Researcher Shah. He is concerned about the impact of the China Pakistan Economic Corridor on local or regional subversion, and the effect on national security policies. Shah is also concerned about other limitations which might prevent BRI from being mired in structural and economic difficulties. He concludes:

> Making BRI a truly win-win and sustainable arrangement, therefore, requires certain precautionary measures to be adopted. Transparency in economic dealings, concern for the impacts (both positive and negative) of massive funding on local economies and institutions and compliance with 'governance-related conditionalities' even if at minimal level are some of the essential prerequisites that China should consider while pursuing BRI project.

Mutual respect for the actual situation of all parties would make the task of Pakistan's incoming government more secure.

Xiao Yunru (China): Integrity

Author and cultural commentator Xiao Yunru writes from Xi'an city, along the ancient Silk Road. He stresses the moral importance of integrity in constructing the BRI (Xiao, 2015). Professor Xiao writes that the BRI will not only be a test of Chinese "hard power", but also a test of China's "soft power" of culture and spirit. The BRI will test the moral level of the Chinese government, of Chinese enterprises, and of the whole people.

For Professor Xiao, this moral credibility will be evident in many fields. He stresses credibility in quality and argues that a veneer of integrity or sub-standard production will expose short-sighted behavior, bringing only loss of trust. Professor Xiao writes that, because BRI incorporates many risks, it must be based on mutual trust and understanding. Trust also underpins the legal relationship of contract. For the market to operate, good will is not sufficient. There must be legally binding contracts which the parties will implement sincerely and credibly.

Professor Xiao links integrity with the legal system. He concludes that his readers need to not only develop integrity as a commercial spirit, and he also links integrity with compliance with laws and regulations, and with integrity in contracting, to the profit of both the state and individuals.

Peter Maurer (Switzerland): Humanity

In May 2017, the Chinese government hosted a Belt and Road Forum in Beijing. The Forum included six thematic sessions held in parallel:

(i) Policy communication, (ii) connectivity of infrastructure, (iii) trade facilitation, (iv) financial cooperation mechanisms, (v) people-to-people exchange, and (vi) think-tank communication. The Red Cross and Red Crescent movement is well established in the BRI countries, including China. The Chinese government invited Dr. Peter Maurer, President of the International Committee of the Red Cross, and Dr. Maurer pleaded for a humanitarian dimension to the BRI. He said that he was "deeply convinced this initiative should add a humanitarian dimension, which will be an important building-block to deliver on the SDGs [Sustainable Development Goals]" (Maurer, 2017). Dr. Maurer was responding to the emphasis on economics at the Forum, thus linking the Red Cross's work in humanitarian relief with the overall goals of the BRI.

Chan Chun Sing (Singapore): Trust

Chan Chun Sing is a politician in Singapore, and a senior minister in the Singapore government as Minister of Trade and Industry. Minister Chan attended the Davos Forum in January 2018. In the course of a panel discussion, Minister Chan suggested that BRI gave the Chinese the opportunity to "win the trust and confidence of the world" by lifting their focus from short- and medium-term benefit to long-term benefit for all the participants (Chan, 2018). Minister Chan switched to Chinese to use the term 以德服人 (serving the people through morality) to emphasize that winning the trust and confidence of the world is a form of service, carried out according to morality.

> We should expect moral leadership not only from China and Chinese people, but also from individuals and institutions in all of the BRI countries.

Quoting a traditional saying — the expression translated as "serving the people through morality" comes from Mencius — indicates the importance of incorporating traditional values in modern morality. Modern China is still coming to terms with its ethical traditions, and their relationship with socialist ethics.

An Interim Conclusion

What do we learn about the attributes of moral leadership along the BRI? At the simplest level, we can list the attributes that we have observed: Reciprocity (Önen), Good Governance (Zou), Ethical Credibility (Chang), Transparency (Kassenova), Integrity (Xiao), Respect (Shah), Humanity (Maurer), and Trust (Chan). Further research may identify other attributes of moral leadership. These attributes are not simply to be found in moral theory, but are also the beginning of a practical description. Moreover, these attributes are both contemporary and traditional. Some attributes, such as trust, and honesty are found in Aristotle and Confucius. But other attributes seem more modern: transparency is an attribute which has grown in more open societies, with greater social participation. Perhaps while transparency seems to be a modern attribute, its roots are evident in older concepts such as frankness and honesty.

Asymmetry in Relationships

One important context must be added to all the individual attributes listed above: asymmetry. In the BRI relationships between the parties may not be symmetrical. China is larger and more powerful than its other partners, although smaller partners may be more symmetrical in relationships with each other. Two examples will make this clear. China is providing finance, through loans and grants. A single loan from China may be overwhelming, given the financial capacity of a recipient nation. Researcher Shah has noted that the billions of dollars of investment under CPEC carry "the risk of straining Pakistan's institutions and economy" (Shah, 2018, p. 384). In labor relations, Professor Zou has pointed to the problem of China's investment power compromising the ability of small recipient countries to implement ILO labor standards (Zou, 2016, p. 19).

Handling this asymmetry in relationships has a moral dimension: attributes such as respect and reciprocity may be more difficult to implement in an asymmetrical relationship. Moral leadership carries a responsibility for a very high degree of respect and integrity to enable a positive outcome for all parties.

Conclusion

We can incorporate here the interim conclusions listed above, but we must add the dimension of asymmetry. Because China has initiated the BRI projects, it has already undertaken a type of leadership. Thus most of the responses listed above were directed to China. But BRI is not only a series of bilateral projects, it also is multilateral. We should expect moral leadership not only from China and Chinese people, but also from individuals and institutions in all of the BRI countries. Also, moral leadership faces particular difficulties when the relationship is not symmetrical. The larger party, even without intending to, might overwhelm the smaller parties.

Thinking about moral leadership is not limited to moral theory. We may legitimately have expectations of what moral leadership might be in practice. The attributes listed here are a beginning for a description. Encountering local people along the Belt and Road and searching in their responses for the attributes of moral leadership may have a theoretical dimension, but it is primarily practical for the large proportion of humanity within its ambit.

References

Cai, P. (2017). Understanding China's Beltand Road Initiative. Lowy Institute. Retrieved from https://www.lowyinstitute.org/sites/default/files/documents/ Understanding%20China%E2%80%99s%20Belt%20and%20Road%20 Initiative_WEB_1.pdf.

Chan, C. (2018). The Belt and Road impact. Podcast Retrieved from https://www. youtube.com/watch?v=cqF64MiYwzE (the relevant passage is at approximately 42 minutes through the discussion).

Chang, P. (6 June 2018). How China lost sight of Malaysia's changes: China's ethical missteps in Malaysia offer lessons for the Belt and Road. *The Diplomat*. Retrieved from www.thediplomat.com/2018/06/how-china-lost-sight-of-malaysias-changes/.

Communique. (16 May 2017). Joint communique of the leaders roundtable of the Belt and Road forum for international cooperation. Retrieved from https:// www.fmprc.gov.cn/mfa_eng/zxxx_662805/t1462012.shtml.

Kassenova, N. (26 February 2018). Information on the projects should be available to the public. *FES-Connect*. Retrieved from https://www.fes-connect.org/ news-detail/information-on-the-projects-should-be-available-to-the-public/.

Liu, C. and Sukumaran, T. (30 July 2017). Belt and Read: How China is exporting education and influence to Malaysia and other Asean countries. *South China Morning Post*. Retrieved from https://www.scmp.com/week-asia/ politics/article/2097965/belt-road-and-books-how-chinas-trying-soft-power-outreach.

Maurer, P. (15 May 2017). Why there should be a humanitarian dimension to China's Belt and Road Project. *International Committee of the Red Cross*. Retrieved from https://www.icrc.org/en/document/humanitarian-dimension-belt-and-road-initiative.

Önen, A. (20 November 2017). Belt and Road Project to boost Turkish economy, new envoy to China says. *Daily Sabah*. Retrieved from https://www.dailysabah.com/ economy/2017/11/20/belt-and-road-project-to-boost-turkish-economy-new-envoy-to-china-says-1511345526.

Shah, A. (2018). How does China-Pakistan economic corridor show the limitations of China's 'One Belt One Road' Model. *Asia and the Pacific Policy Studies*, 5(2), 378–385. https://onlinelibrary.wiley.com/doi/full/10.1002/ app5.224.

Xi, J. (8 September 2013). Promote friendship between our people and work together to build a bright future. Retrieved from https://www.fmprc.gov.cn/ mfa_eng/wjdt_665385/zyjh_665391/t1078088.shtml.

Xiao, Y. (3 August 2015). Integrity is the moral cornerstone for building One Belt One Road. *Xian Evening Daily*. Retrieved from www.xiancn.com/zt/ content/2015-08/04/content_3017884.htm. 肖云儒: 诚信是建设 "一带一路"的道德基石 "西安新闻网-西安晚报"

Xinhua. (28 March 2015a). China unveils action plan on Belt and Road Initiative. Retrieved from http://english.gov.cn/news/top_news/2015/03/28/content_ 281475079055789.htm.

Xinhua. (29 March 2015b). Full text: Vision and actions on jointly building Belt and Road. Retrieved from http://english.cri.cn/12394/2015/03/29/ 2941s872030.htm.

Zou, M. (2016). Labor standards along One Belt One Road. In Lutz-Christian Wolff and Chao Xi (eds.), *Legal Dimensions of China's Belt and Road Initiative.* Hong Kong: Wolters Kluwer.

Social Innovation

Chapter 10

Angel or Demon? The Ethics of Online Peer-to-Peer Lending Firms[*]

Helen Xu

RA Supervisor, RB China, Beijing
Beijing Reckitt (China) Holding Company, Ltd.

Abstract

Online Peer-to-Peer (P2P) lending schemes began to flourish in China in 2015. This lending model, where lender and borrower could do transactions without involving banking institutions, was welcomed by many start-ups and entrepreneurs because it provided an effective solution for reaching borrowers directly. One of these borrower classes was college students. Campus loans, facilitated through P2P platforms, quickly became popular. However, after a series of university scandals, questions emerged as to the morality of the industry and the responsibility of the P2P platforms within it to guard against abuses inflicted upon college students and the borrower market as a whole.

---

[*]This chapter originally appeared in *Macau Ricci Institute Journal*, June 2018, Issue 2, pp. 69–79. A shorter version of this essay was published as a case study, "The ethics of online lending firms — Good or evil?" in S. Rothlin, D. McCann, and P. Haghirian (Eds.), *Doing Good Business in China*, Singapore: World Scientific Press, 2021, pp. 63–71.

Alipay, a part of Ant Financial Service Group (Ant Financial, n.d.), is one of the leading third-party online payment platforms in China. It was launched in 2004 and has become widely known for its integration of a variety of consumer-oriented features, including "payment, lifestyle service, civil services, social networking, wealth management, insurance and public welfare". It also boasted "over 450 million registered users and 200 financial institution partners" as of June, 2016 (Ant Family, n.d.).

Since its inception Alipay has produced a number of software updates for its smartphone application. At the launch of Alipay 9.0, a financing platform titled, "I Owe You (IOU)", was introduced. It was well received among younger generations, especially those at university and working far away from their hometowns. To use IOU, the only requirement is that the lender and borrower are mutual "friends" — for example, on WeChat, or a related Chinese social media application. Once friendship status is established, the steps for acquiring a loan are as follows:

1. Choose the friend you would like to ask for a loan.
2. Choose the IOU function.
3. Fill in a form, including information on the amount to be borrowed, period of repayment, suggested interest rate, and purpose of the funds.
4. Send the form to the friend specified in step 1 until the money you've required is transferred into your account (Roy, 2015).

However, after nine months of operation, Alipay terminated its IOU function. Why? On 9 March 2016, a sophomore in Henan Province, going by the alias of "Zheng Xu", committed suicide because he was unable to pay back the money he had borrowed (RMB 600,000 in total) from several online lending firms, Alipay's IOU among them. Zheng, having come from a poor, agrarian background, was a model student in secondary school. It came as a shock to find out he had compiled such a massive debt, and even involved 28 of his classmates in his borrowing activity. Zheng's borrowing came to an unfortunate conclusion when, feeling depressed and hopeless under the weight of the debt, he left a final message to his family before ending his life:

> As a son of yours, I feel very sorry to you. But I'm not up to [living anymore], especially when I found [that all of my efforts in life were in vain].... I heard that jumping from the building may feel very painful, but I'm really tired! I do appreciate your help and the meticulous care you showed me as always, and I'm so sorry to all of you (Hu, 2016).

After Zheng's suicide, Chen Zijun, a lawyer from Shanghai, mentioned that the rise of peer-to-peer (P2P) lending practices on college campuses posed real challenges, both ethical and legal, and currently lacked substantial regulation:

> According to the *Interim Measures for the Administration of Personal Loans*, the personal loans shall be in accordance with the legal compliance, principle of prudent operation, equality, voluntary, fairness and sincerity. In consideration of the particularity of college students, the legislation shall take into full account their repayment capacity, enhance a healthy consumption concept and protect their lawful rights and interests. It was in response to Zheng's death that Alipay removed its IOU function from its list of services (Hu, 2016).

But not for long. Several days after it was removed, the Ministry of Education and the Chinese Banking Regulatory Commission issued its *Notification on Strengthening the Risk Prevention and Educational Guidance of Bad Online Lending Practice on Campus*, which requires "colleges and universities to establish a monitoring and precautionary system to protect students from the schemes of irregular online lending firms" (Tang, 2016). Since August, 2016, Alipay's IOU function has been back in operation. Another P2P lending platform, Jiedaibao, was established by Kunwu Jiuding Capital Holdings Co. Ltd. Like Alipay, Jiedaibao has a relatively basic loan approval process, but claims to go further in terms of privacy, especially for the lender. Lenders on Jiedaibao enjoy what the firm calls "unidirectional anonymity", which prohibits the borrowers from knowing from whom their loans are originating. This operational model was praised by the industry and garnered a number of awards, including the Annual Most Influential Brand by the 2015 Global Mobile Internet CEO Summit, the New Financial Service Award by the *National Business Daily*, and The Most Innovative APP in Financial Field by the *CNR News* (Jiedaibao, n.d.).

However, Jiedaibao found itself at the center of controversy at the end of November, 2016, when a substantial number of nude pictures and videos were leaked online (CnBeta, 2016). The pictures and videos were collected as a substitute for instalments on loans borrowed by (mostly) female college students. The *China Daily* reported:

> Many Chinese university students were found to have used their nude pictures as IOUs on some online lending platforms, putting themselves

at risk of having everybody — including their parents — see them naked (Jiang, 2016).

It was also reported that some lenders were charging inordinately high interest rates, 1,564 percent being one of the highest, which may have contributed to the fact that these women could not pay their instalments. These revelations created a public outcry. A collection of sentiments from Chinese social media is set out below:

> I will never ever understand such behaviours taken by female students who took nude picture in order to borrow one or two thousand yuan, while some of them lent out one thousand yuan at an excessive rate of interest. […] Most of college students are adults, who had to learn to take responsibility for their own mistakes. Meanwhile, they must stand out for rights violation. — Dianfeng Juanke (He, 2017)

> Taking nude pictures for loan revealed a crucial point of social reality that for young ladies of those pictures, the indignity of being poor has now far exceeded the indignity of being naked — this feeling forced them to put their entire privacy and networking at risk for [a few] thousand yuan. — Caiwang (He, 2017)

> Their 'buy first, pay later' idea was easy to sell. Credit service users could choose between delayed payments and repayments in instalments. Students need to spend just five minutes to fill in the consumer credit application online. — *China Daily* (Jiang, 2016)

In response to the resulting outrage, Jiedaibao posted an official statement clarifying their position:

> Jiedaibao is an online P2P lending platform adhering to the principle of lawfulness and compliance. The company [claims] no responsibility [or ownership] for the nude pictures. These inappropriate photos came from private deals between users and third parties through irregular operations.… Concerning the spreading of nude pictures online, the Department of Legal Affairs has collected the relevant evidence and already reported this to the responsible public security organ. We intend to take legal actions to crack down on the persons responsible for the

illegal lending practices and for [Disseminating the nude photographs] (CnBeta, 2016).

P2P lending, which is an offshoot of a more general borrowing trend on college campuses,[1] is becoming more popular among students. Quick access to cash without the barriers that traditional banks impose, on the one hand, gives students more freedom of choice at university. On the other, however, it can be a temptation that smothers one in debt. Such a situation can result in tragedies like those aforementioned. According to a survey distributed by Beijing Zhicheng Credit Service Co. Ltd., in April, 2015, 78 percent of college students responded that they experienced a shortage of funds either frequently or occasionally. 2.6 percent of respondents reportedly applied for microcredits and 8.6 percent indicated that they investigated online P2P firms. 15.5 percent stated they addressed their financial shortcoming through traditional bank loans (Zou, 2016). Another survey, within the *Consumption Report of Online P2P Lending in College Students*, revealed that 29 percent of respondents applied for loans, of which over 60 percent obtained financing through a P2P platform (Jin, 2017).

As P2P lending grows in prevalence, questions are emerging as to the responsibilities of platforms such as Alipay and Jiedaibao to their users, both lenders and borrowers. Given their role as intermediaries who simply provide the means for lenders and borrowers to facilitate financing transactions, are they absolved from responsibility if, for example, lenders engage in predatory practices? Are they responsible if lenders, for example, begin demanding nude photos from female borrowers? Or if

> Critics suggest that companies like Alipay and Jiedaibao ought to engage in proactive self-governance instead of waiting for either government regulations to catch up or a public scandal to force a reactionary adjustment.

---

[1] Other types of credit acquired by university students include shopping loans offered by shopping platforms, credit lines offered by companies such as Taobao and JD, and micro-loans offered by traditional banks.

lenders are charging over 1,000 percent interest? The basic requirement for entering into a financing transaction using Alipay's IOU is that lender and borrower be "friends". This assumes that, by virtue of their status as "friends", the parties will carry out their exchanges within reason, and without exposing one or the other party to undue risk.

The examples above show how lenders can abuse borrowers. But given the rather sketchy requirements for borrowers to obtain financing, there is also the possibility of lenders being taken advantage of, especially because companies like Alipay and Jiedaibao do not guarantee the loans transacted on their platforms. There is good reason for this. In August 2015, the Supreme People's Court of China ruled that "online P2P lending platforms who offer guarantee for the loan shall bear the responsibility for bond" (Article 22) (Supreme People's Court, 2015). In other words, Alipay and Jiedaibao do not have much incentive to guarantee loans, given the risk of having to assume liability for loan defaults.

Another area of concern is whether Alipay and Jiedaibao are enabling predatory lenders to exploit needy borrowers, due to their all-too-easy requirements for borrowers obtaining credit. The four steps for obtaining a loan through Alipay's IOU couldn't be more basic and reveal nothing of the borrower's credit history or current financial standing. This can put borrowers — and potentially their families — in desperate situations if they borrow more than they can repay. Perhaps that is why, in April, 2017, the China Banking Regulatory Commissions declared that "offering online lending service to college students under 18 years old is prohibited" (Jin, 2017). This is likely because young, uninformed borrowers are at a higher risk of entering into financing agreements they are unable to uphold, and thereby at a higher risk of being sued, or worse exploited, by unsympathetic lenders.

A parallel example of how a platform might allow predatory behavior is Baidu. Their Tieba forums were the cause of scandal, when in 2016 the company began bidding out the administration of its disease-related forums — that is, the ability to monitor and manage the content of exchanges — to unlicensed private hospitals, unqualified doctors and pharmaceutical companies. This decision allowed predatory, for-profit organizations to begin pushing their own products and services to the users of the forums. The result? Many users who decided to buy the products or procure the services soon found out that either the offers were fabricated or not at all what they expected. In other words, Baidu was the platform through which exploitative exchanges were being facilitated. Public outrage eventually forced Baidu's hand, and they altered their policies to curb the abuse; but the damage was done. Similar responses are becoming increasingly common in the P2P industry. Critics suggest that companies like Alipay and Jiedaibao ought to engage in proactive self-governance instead of waiting for either government regulations to catch up or a public scandal to force a reactionary adjustment.

A related area of concern surrounds the idea of disclosure. In the *Consumption Report of Online P2P Lending for College Students*, 68 percent of college students reported that they received less than RMB 1,500 per month for living expenses, mostly from their parents. This has caused students to look for additional sources of income, one of those sources being P2P companies. However, P2P companies seem to have done a poor job ensuring that new borrowers are well informed of their debt obligations. For example, in the study cited above, only 22 percent of those who borrowed money "understood the terms of loans well" (Jin, 2017). This is a major problem, because had they understood the terms of their loans thoroughly, they may not have gone through with it in the first place.

Perhaps at this point Confucius' teaching should be recalled:

Wealth and high rank are what people desire; if they are attained by not following the *dao*, do not dwell in them. Poverty and mean rank are what people hate; if they cannot be overcome by following the *dao*, do not depart from them (*Confucius*, 2015, p. 14).

Building on this wisdom, a commentary from *Netease* on the P2P phenomenon on college campuses in China stated that:

A normal financial ecology on campus means that: college students take their own responsibility for the debt default; financial institutions who issue irregular loans bear the loss by itself; the financial supervisory departments offer financial education and punish the abusive mortgage lenders in a timely fashion (Nie, 2016).

As P2P lending grows and becomes more prevalent, what can pioneer platforms like Alipay and Jiedaibao do to help prevent the kind of tragedies and abuses described above?

- Proactively work with the Chinese government to develop consumer-centric industry regulations: Firms like Alipay and Jiedaibao bring valuable industry experience that can help regulatory agencies develop appropriate guidelines for the marketplace. This is advantageous because the firms who contribute to this process will not, except in cases of wilful disregard, find themselves in trouble with the law. It also sends a message to their consumers that their best interests are being taken to heart and that they want to be compliant, transparent, and fair. This kind of behavior creates win-win outcomes for all stakeholders involved.
- Offer values education to college students: As P2P lending becomes popular on university campuses in China, there is an opportunity for leading companies like Alipay and Jiedaibao to educate prospective borrowers about the risks involved in obtaining financing. Informing borrowers about predatory lending, illegal loan outlets, interest rates and amortization tables, and living within one's means will not only create better and more responsible borrowers, but also position certain brands as trustworthy authorities within an industry. The more trust a firm demands from the market, the more likely they will be top of mind when prospective borrowers begin searching for credit. Firms could conduct values education by setting up on-campus lectures or workshops, or offering a live hotline for borrowers to learn about financing and the specific risks facing them as students.
- Partner with universities to provide scholarships or related aid: If Alipay, for example, wanted to offer services to a university, then they could provide incentives, such as scholarships, to students in need as a means of promotion and brand building. This would encourage the university to do its due diligence, to ensure they are not promoting exploitative platforms to their students, while incentivizing the platforms to hold themselves accountable to strict standards of excellence, so as not to tarnish their image amongst target markets.
- Setting standards of excellence in the industry: P2P lending firms would be wise to target those borrowers who can demonstrate an ability to repay their debts. Establishing a more robust qualification process will weed out unlikely borrowers and assure lenders that their borrowers will make good on their loans. This is win-win. It allows borrowers to acquire needed cash and lenders to make money from interest payments. It protects borrowers from entering into lending situations they don't fully understand and prevents lenders from

exploiting gullible borrowers. It hedges against scandal and promotes sustainability.

The regulatory environment for the P2P industry in China is still developing. Significant ambiguity exists concerning how P2P companies should operate their platforms. Given this, in May, 2017 the China Banking Regulatory Commission (CBRC), Central Committee of the Communist Youth League and Ministry of Education jointly released a regulatory notice stipulating a series of restrictions on P2P companies and requiring local authority and banking institutions to adopt measures to put an end to financial exploitation on university campuses (China Banking Regulatory Commission, 2017). At the same time, the central government has begun monitoring the source of campus loans and prohibiting P2P lending firms from offering credit services to college students without the approval of the CBRC.

One counter to the abuses within the P2P industry, particularly as practiced in university settings, is financial education. The first Chinese platform dedicated to such education, "Practical Money Skills", was co-developed by Visa Greater China and the China Financial Literacy Education Synergy Innovation Center at Beijing Normal University in 2017. Then CEO of Visa, Shirley Yu-Tsui, considered it "a meaningful attempt in the field of digital financial education" (Sina, 2017). The platform was designed to "equip people worldwide with money management tools and resources". Given the company's expertise in financial services, Visa Greater China was able to help "individuals and communities to build healthy futures by receiving interactive tools and educational resources". They did this through online learning and through commercial banks who would reach out to local colleges and universities to provide a range of financial literacy services, including teach-ins, forums, and training seminars. One example of the latter was the launch of, "Introducing Financial Literacy to Campus", an initiative developed by 62 universities and 35 Chinese-funded commercial banks in Shanghai in response to the lack of such resources on university campuses in China (Lin, 2017). Many well-renowned financial institutions participated, including the China Construction Bank Shanghai Branch, Shanghai Pudong Development Bank, and Industrial Bank Co. Ltd. Similar initiatives have been launched in Beijing as well. For example, the Bank of Communications Beijing Branch developed a series of financial literacy lectures, which were integrated into curriculums at Beijing Forestry University (The Beijing News,

2017). Likewise, the Banking Association of Guangdong carried out promotional campaigns focusing on the dangers of bad loans and irresponsible borrowing (Li, 2016).

It is promising to see China's financial institutions responding to the central government's call to reduce abuse and increase knowledge about financial literacy on China's university campuses. For P2P companies, this knowledge will result in more prudent borrowers and more honest lenders. Paired with the commendable and ongoing efforts of China's authorities in developing responsible regulations for the P2P industry, there is hope for reform, the rebuilding of trust and the shaping of P2P practices toward the common good.

References

Ant Family. (n.d.). Ant financial. Retrieved from https://www.antfin.com/family.htm.

CnBeta. (2016). 借贷宝发布关于网传借贷宝不雅照泄漏的公告. [Jiexibao issued an announcement on the leak of indecent photos of Jiexibao online]. Retrieved from https://www.cnbeta.com/articles/tech/563153.htm.

China Banking Regulatory Commission. (2017). 中国银监会、共青团中央、教育部关于开展送金融知识进校园活动的通知. [Notice of the China Banking Regulatory Commission, the Central Committee of the Communist Youth League and the Ministry of Education on Carrying out the Activities of Popularizing Financial Knowledge to Campus]. Retrieved from http://www.cbrc.gov.cn/govView_2146132E50494922AD8010E22550184B.html.

Confucius. (2015). *The Analects of Confucius*. Retrieved from http://www.indiana.edu/~p374/ Analects_of_Confucius_(Eno-2015).pdf.

Eno, R. and He, X. T. (Trans.) (2017). 女大学生借5000元滚成26万元, 裸贷何时休?昨天, 银监会出手了.[The female college student borrowed RMB5,000 and turned it into RMB260,000. When will the naked loan stop? The China Banking Regulatory Commission took action]. *Sina*. Retrieved from http://finance.sina.com.cn/wm/2017-04-11/doc-ifyeayzu7529285.shtml.

Hu, J. F. Y. (2016). 学生负债自杀案令人惊恐, 校园借贷为何失控 [Student debt suicide case is horrifying, why campus borrowing is out of control]. *Sohu*. Retrieved from http://mt.sohu.com/20160320/n441212293.shtml.

Jiang, J. (2016). Nude pics as IOU: A new, risky online loan among Chinese university students. *China Daily*. Retrieved from http://www.chinadaily.com.cn/china/2016-07/14/content_26089898.htm.

Jiang, X. Q. (2016). Careless on the Chinese campus. *China Daily*. Retrieved from http://africa.chinadaily.com.cn/business/2016-09/26/content_26893195.htm.

Jiedaibao. (n.d.). *Jiedaibao*. Retrieved from http://www.jiedaibao.com/.

Jin, J. (2017). 校园网贷 诱人馅饼还是吃人陷阱? [Online loan at campus, a tempting pie or cannibalistic trap?]. *Tencent*. Retrieved from https://finance. qq.com/a/20170411/034929.htm.

Li, W. S. (2016). 广东银行业"普及金融知识万里行"活动隆重启动, [The Guangdong Banking Industry launched "Popularizing Financial Knowledge" activities], *Sohu*. Retrieved from http://www.sohu.com/a/76713774_362056.

Lin, F. Y. (2017). 上海银行业青年"送金融知识进校园"活动全面启动. [The activity of "Popularizing Financial Knowledge to Campus" for Shanghai Banking Youths was fully launched], *CNR*. Retrieved from http://www.cnr.cn/ shanghai/tt/20170616/t20170616_523805446.shtml.

Nie, R. M. (2016). "校园贷"不能一刀切, 但"高利贷"得有人管. [Stopping "campus loan" is not a one-size-fits-all solution, but "usury issue" has to be solved]. *NetEase*. Retrieved from http://money.163.com/16/0317/11/ BIBSMQUE00253B0H.html?baike.

Practical Money Skills. (n.d.). About. Retrieved from http://www.practical moneyskills.com/about/recognition.

Roy. (2015). 支付宝可打借条?小编教你电子借条怎么用. [Can Alipay make IOUs? A tutorial on how to use electronic IOUs]. *PConline*. Retrieved from http://pcedu.pconline.com.cn/667/6676896.html.

Sina. (2017). Visa 发布国内首个"实用理财技巧"金融教育网站. [Visa publishes China's 1st Financial Education Website to popularizing "Practical Financial Tips"]. *Sina*. Retrieved from http://gongyi.sina.com.cn/gyzx/2017-09-01/doc-ifykpysa2451113.shtml.

Supreme People's Court. (2015). 最高人民法院关于审理民间借贷案件适用法律若干问题的规定. [Provisions of the Supreme People's Court on Several Issues concerning the Application of Law in the Trial of Private Lending Cases]. Retrieved from http://www.court.gov.cn/fabu-xiangqing-15146.html.

Tang, X. L. (2016). 又是裸条, 又是自杀, 校园贷款把大学生逼上绝路. [Naked IOUs and suicides, campus loans drove college students to a dead end]. *Sohu*. Retrieved from http://view.163.com/16/0816/00/BUI4BGM3 000159OQ.html.

The Beijing News. (2017). 交行北京分行走进北京林业大学. [Bank of Communications Beijing Branch launched activities at Beijing Forestry University]. *Sohu*. Retrieved from http://www.sohu.com/a/193925378_ 114988.

Zou, C. S. (15). 图解: 大学生网贷现况调查报告. [Survey Report on the Current Situation of College Students' Online Loans]. *Southcn.com*. Retrieved from http://tech.southcn.com/t/2016-08/15/content_153644135.htm.

https://doi.org/10.1142/9789811250231_0011

Chapter 11

Police Cooperation and the Fight Against Cross-Border Crime Among Belt and Road Countries: The Emergence and Proliferation of Telecommunication Fraud in Greater China*

Sonny Shiu-Hing Lo

*Deputy Director, Arts and Sciences, HKU Space,
University of Hong Kong*

Abstract

Instances of telecommunication fraud in the region of Greater China — the People's Republic of China (PRC), Hong Kong, Macao and Taiwan — have increased since 2015. Some criminal elements involved in telecommunication fraud have been operating in Belt and Road countries outside either the PRC or Taiwan. The governments of Greater China have been cooperating to combat telecommunication fraud. This paper examines the pattern of telecommunication fraud and addresses the issue of how the governments of China and Taiwan have been tackling it in cooperation with the countries involved in the Belt and Road Initiative (BRI).

---

*This chapter originally appeared in *Macau Ricci Institute Journal*, June, 2019, Issue 4, pp. 40–50.

Introduction

The BRI has brought about an unprecedented degree of human interaction across national boundaries; nevertheless, a challenge to the BRI is the spread of cross-border criminal activities. Cross-border crimes can be seen as a result of the liberalization of border control; they are exacerbated by the greediness of criminal organizations and, to some extent, bureaucratic corruption in law enforcement (Lo, 2009). This paper will explore how police cooperation in the fight against cross-border crime has been playing a significant role in the development and prospects of countries participating in the BRI. Apart from utilizing the BRI as a platform to strengthen economic and diplomatic relations with various countries in the world, the PRC also hopes to consolidate security relations with them (Brown, 2018, p. 215). Traditionally, China has cooperated with many countries along the BRI to fight against various types of crimes, such as smuggling, drug trafficking and terrorism. In recent years, the joint efforts made by China and many other countries to combat telecommunication fraud have become more urgent with the rising popularity of the Internet. This digital aspect is becoming a hallmark of cross-border crime control between China and many BRI countries. With the increased cooperation between the Chinese police and their counterparts of various countries, the prospects for the BRI in consolidating multilateral trade and cultural-social as well as economic linkages remain optimistic. Efforts at fighting cross-border telecommunication fraud include intelligence gathering and sharing among law enforcement agencies, reports from the mass media, and the vigilance of the citizens who are the victims of such crimes. The persistence of these efforts can and will contribute to the success of the BRI.

The Rise of Telecommunication Fraud in Greater China

Telecommunication fraud recently has surged in the region of Greater China. From 2011 to April 2015, police in China and their Taiwanese counterparts actually arrested 7,700 Chinese people from both places, with approximately 4,600 of the 7,700 arrested coming from Taiwan. In May 2015, for instance, 32 Taiwanese criminal suspects who had made calls from a Malaysia-based telecommunication fraud syndicate were arrested by the Malaysian authorities. But the Taiwanese were handed back to the law enforcement authorities of the PRC rather than to the Republic of China (ROC) in Taiwan. Some Taiwan people argued that the Taiwanese should be sent back to the island republic rather than to the Mainland. However, the PRC police contended that since most of the victims were Mainlanders, and 50 percent of the losses were due to Taiwanese-led syndicates, those detained should face trial in the PRC.

In another case, in November 2015, the PRC police cooperated with their counterparts in Indonesia, Hong Kong and Taiwan to arrange the return of 254 Mainland Chinese criminal suspects involved in a huge cross-border telecommunication fraud syndicate (Mai, 2015). Ninety people in Guangdong province were arrested, including seven Taiwanese. Working from bases in Indonesia and the Philippines, they cheated citizens of Hong Kong and Taiwan by making calls to the Chinese in both places, pretending that they were PRC police officers and claiming that the

Efforts at fighting cross-border telecommunication fraud include intelligence gathering and sharing among law enforcement agencies, reports from the mass media, and the vigilance of the citizens who are the victims of such crimes.

victims had committed criminal offences, as a pretext for demanding monetary compensation. The money stolen by the Taiwanese syndicate went to Taiwan-based bank accounts. In March 2016, PRC police uncovered another extortion plot in which a 50-year-old man had lost RMB 2.7 billion, through a telephone fraud in which scammers falsely accused him of laundering dirty money for which they held an arrest warrant against him. His funds also found their way to a Taiwanese account.

These are typical of the numerous examples of cross-border telecommunication fraud. Several characteristics are prominent. First and foremost, the criminals often operate from bases outside the PRC and Taiwan so that law enforcement authorities in both places cannot arrest them easily. Second, when the Taiwanese suspects are arrested, the PRC government often requests that they, along with Mainland Chinese criminal suspects, should be sent back to the PRC for trial because the victims of telecommunication fraud are mainly from the PRC. While most third countries have sent back all the criminal suspects to the PRC, including both Mainland and Taiwan Chinese, the Taiwan authorities naturally hope that Taiwanese suspects should be sent directly to Taiwan.

In August 2016, five Taiwanese criminal suspects were declared by a Kenya court to be not guilty of telecommunication fraud, but surprisingly they were later sent back to Mainland China, leading to a complaint from the Taiwan foreign ministry (*Apple Daily*, 2016: A19). The Taiwan government also asked its PRC counterpart to report on the personal safety of the five Taiwanese in accordance with the 2009 agreement between the PRC and ROC governing the custody of cross-border criminal suspects. Yet, in response to Taiwan's concern, PRC authorities dismissed the request, contending that the new Taiwan government under the presidency of Tsai Ing-wen should do more to resume the communication channels between the two sides.

Responses from Taiwan and the PRC

Despite the sour relations reflecting renewed tensions between the PRC and the Taiwan governments on how to handle Taiwanese people being arrested by a third country, both governments have recently taken strong measures to deal with cross-border criminal activities. In November 2016, the Taiwan Legislative Yuan revised Article 5 of the Criminal Law (*Criminal Code of the Republic of China*, 2018), adding more legal penalties for Taiwanese citizens who commit crimes through their participation in cross- border telecommunication fraud. Those people convicted of serious offenses under this law can be imprisoned for 20 years maximum. The term "cross-border criminal fraud" was also added to Article 5, authorizing the judicial authorities not only to impose stiffer penalties but also to take jurisdiction over the management of these criminal suspects. Nevertheless, empowering the judicial authorities to have such jurisdiction is one thing; whether the PRC authorities and the third countries will allow the Taiwan government to exercise that jurisdiction appears to be another matter.

Meanwhile, the PRC authorities have also increased the penalties for telecommunication fraud. On December 20, 2016, a legal document issued by the Supreme People's Court, the Supreme People's Procuratorate and the Ministry of Public Security proposed that offenders convicted of telecommunication fraud amounting to or exceeding 3,000 yuan would be imprisoned for a minimum of three years, and that those offenders cheating other people for any amount over 500,000 yuan would be imprisoned indefinitely (*China Daily*, 2016: 5). Obviously, internet crime has become so serious in the PRC that the criminal courts and police authorities have to adopt stringent measures to curb its growth.

Nevertheless, since Taiwan has diplomatic relations with relatively few countries in the world, extradition of criminal suspects involved in telecommunication fraud directly from the country concerned to Taiwan remains difficult. Many Taiwanese criminal suspects try to exploit the loophole resulting from Taiwan's lack of extradition agreements with many countries in the world. However, some Taiwanese criminal suspects involved in telecommunication fraud have received imprisonment sentences from the countries where they started the fraud operation. For example, in February 2018, four Taiwanese who were arrested in Thailand for engaging in telecommunication fraud and money laundering were imprisoned for 16 years and six months in Thailand — a heavy penalty that could act as a deterrent to Taiwan criminal suspects (*Ta Kung Pao*, 2018a: A19).

For countries that do not have diplomatic relations with Taipei, in cases where Taiwanese criminal suspects stand accused of telecommunication frauds involving Mainland Chinese, the PRC requested that the accused be sent directly to the PRC for trial. In December 2017, the PRC government formally requested that the South Korean government should extradite 51 Taiwanese criminal suspects in a telecommunication fraud, which cheated not only Taiwanese but also Mainland Chinese (*Ming Pao*, 2017: A11).

One challenge in the struggle against telecommunication fraud is that many Taiwanese involved in telecommunication fraud are young people, who have taken the risk of getting rich by participating in such activities. In 2016, 71.77 percent of the 21,576 Taiwan residents who committed telecommunication fraud in the island republic were from the age group between 18 and 39 (*Ta Kung Pao*, 2018a).

If the PRC is keen to promote its model of good governance to other countries along the BRI, then there are grounds for optimism in the struggle against cross-border telecommunication fraud, which is in the common interest of all countries along the BRI, and in the world.

The PRC government recognizes the severity of telecommunication fraud and has taken immediate measures to address it. On 18 and 19 April 2018, State Councillor and Minister of Public Security Zhao Kezhi chaired a nationwide conference in Shenzhen on combatting crime, including telecommunication fraud. Many public security chiefs attended as he emphasized the need for the utilization of artificial intelligence and big data to fight crime (*Sing Tao Daily*, 2018: A24). President Xi Jinping also held a meeting on 20 and 21 April to follow up on the conference, emphasizing the importance of internet security, the need for education of the netizens, and the importance of self-discipline among internet webmasters and professionals in cooperation with the government to fight internet crime.

A New Pattern

Recently, a new pattern of telecommunication fraud has emerged in the Greater China region, including: (1) manufactured love affairs, (2) investment fraud, and (3) tax evasion and related money laundering activities. In Hong Kong, from 2010 to 2018, for example, a rich woman was cheated by her so-called "lover" through the Internet, causing her to lose a total of HK$1.4 million via remittances to Malaysia. In October 2018, the police in Hong Kong, Malaysia and Singapore smashed a telecommunication fraud syndicate that recruited 52 people from the three places to disguise themselves as actors, footballers, professionals, military officers and rich people, cheating mostly Chinese women in the Greater China region (*Wen Wei Po*, 2018: A01; *Ta Kung Pao*, 2018b: A04). The 28 Hong Kong people arrested in this ring opened accounts in Hong Kong to facilitate the process of money laundering after the victims sent their money to the syndicate. After securing the trust of their victims, syndicate members got the details of their credit cards and account information, and in the 147 cases stole a total amount of almost HK$110 million.

Investment fraud and tax evasion are also commonplace in the operation of telecommunication fraud syndicates. In August 2018, the PRC authorities cracked down on tax evasion by celebrities, including Fan Bingbing, who opened studios and empty shell companies in Korgas in Xinjiang. Many of these studios and companies were suspected of being involved in large-scale money laundering, even though the film industry was trying to expand into the west through the BRI.

Implications for BRI Development

The rapid growth of telecommunication fraud within the Greater China region has become the most prominent challenge in combatting cross-border crime. It necessitates frequent cooperation among the police in Greater China (Lo, 2018). Whether stronger penalties can stem the tide of telecommunication fraud remains unclear, but it is certain that education of all the citizens in the regions of Greater China has begun so that the number of victims can and will be minimized. While education of ordinary citizens is easier in both Hong Kong and Macao, the same measures may not be effective in the relatively vast and diverse geographical areas of China and, to some extent, Taiwan. As such, the PRC relies on technological advancement, such as the mobilization of Big Data, to assist its police force in cracking down on telecommunication fraud syndicates.

Of course, education alone cannot curb telecommunication fraud in the era of globalization and regionalization culminating in the development of the BRI. Fortunately, cross-border police cooperation between the PRC and Hong Kong on the one hand and other foreign states on the other hand has succeeded in mitigating the spread of telecommunication fraud in the era of the BRI. The high tide of telecommunication fraud took place in 2016 and its crackdown began in 2017 until the present. As of early 2019, the incidence of telecommunication fraud appears to have declined. Very few reports on telecommunication fraud have been seen, recently, in the local press. The most probable reason is that, as 2019 represents the seventieth anniversary of the PRC, Beijing hopes to honor the year as a historical symbol of the Chinese Communist Party's success. As such, domestic crime and cross-border crime have to be put under tight control, along with a very aggressive united front campaign targeted at winning the hearts and minds of the people of Hong Kong (Lo, Hung and Loo, 2019). Still, it remains to be seen whether telecommunication fraud will resurge again after 2019.

In the context of security in Greater China, the police in Hong Kong appear to be the most effective in curbing telecommunication fraud, followed by Macao, mainland China and Taiwan. The small physical size of the cities of Hong Kong and Macao means that the police forces can control telecommunication fraud relatively easily. The Macao police have been cooperating with their Zhuhai counterparts to crack down on computer-based schemes to cheat local citizens by imitating the techniques of telecommunication fraud syndicates. The police forces in mainland China are more complex, necessitating cross-provincial and cross-city agreements to share intelligence and work together. Taiwan has realized the severity of telecommunication fraud syndicates that also involve their own citizens. In fact, the Taiwan government and police have also made tremendous efforts at fighting telecommunication fraud within Taiwan, while cooperating with foreign countries and also the PRC to extradite Taiwan criminal suspects. After all, cross-border telecommunication fraud syndicates that involve a large number of Taiwanese have already tarnished the good image of Taiwan. Therefore, it is in the common interest of the four governments in the Greater China region to exert effective control on the emergence and operation of telecommunication fraud syndicates.

From the perspective of the security challenges in and for the BRI, telecommunication fraud constitutes a menace to not only the domestic security of the PRC but also its image in the world. As such, the PRC has taken swift and tough action against criminal elements involved in the telecommunication fraud syndicates, especially the Taiwanese. In the minds of PRC leaders, such syndicates are like the new *heidao* (triads) that threaten the regime security of the Chinese Communist Party. They have undermined the good image of the PRC at a time when President Xi Jinping's BRI is in full swing. They have also been taking advantage of the political tensions between Beijing and Taipei. In short, telecommunication fraud syndicates are seen as the enemies of the PRC government, which can no longer tolerate their existence and operations.

From the perspective of foreign countries where criminal elements from the PRC and Taiwan operate their telecommunication fraud schemes, there is willingness to cooperate with the police forces in the Greater China region to fight these criminal activities. However, such illicit activities might make some foreign countries cast doubts on whether the BRI championed by the PRC can and will be as smooth as it is presented in the official rhetoric. To calm the anxieties of foreign countries, the PRC has already made strenuous efforts at combatting cross-boundary crime, while emphasizing the need for good governance, for example, in anti-corruption work. If the PRC is keen to promote its model of good governance to other countries along the BRI, then there are grounds for optimism in the struggle against cross-border telecommunication fraud, which is in the common interest of all countries along the BRI, and in the world.

Finally, from the broader perspective of fighting transnational organized crime, telecommunication fraud syndicates have displayed unique features. Unlike the traditionally hierarchical and tightly organized nature of crime syndicates like the Italian and American mafia (Cressey, 1997), the syndicates that involve Mainland Chinese and Taiwanese in countries outside Greater China appear to be organized quite loosely and are based on personal networks. As the Chinese attach great importance to the concept of *guanxi* (personal connections), it plays a crucial role in recruiting members to join and operate these criminal syndicates. Yet, since the telecommunication fraud syndicates in Belt and Road countries often involve a mixture of both mainland Chinese and Taiwanese, their composition is relatively loose and their *guanxi* is based on the common objective of making quick profits. Furthermore, these syndicates often target their own ethnic group, the Chinese in their hometowns. While their ethnic target is narrow and focused, the support networks extend to non-Chinese accomplices providing logistical support and bases rather than the key leaders in their organizations. Indeed, these telecommunication fraud syndicates cheat their victims through the Internet by utilizing personal data stolen in the regions of Greater China. Identity theft is commonplace in the regions of Greater China, where many individuals are relatively insensitive to this problem, and where private sector organizations and companies acquire personal data easily without much by way of safeguards to protect their privacy.

As such, the roots of telecommunication fraud syndicates are deep in the regions of Greater China. Their complete elimination may be a bridge too far, but the education of ordinary citizens and private sector organizations on how to protect the personal data of individuals can be a first step toward the prevention of such crime, followed by multiple measures, notably the sharing of criminal intelligence among police forces in Greater China and the persistent cooperation between them and their overseas counterparts.

References

Apple Daily. (2016 August 9), A19.

Brown, K. (2018). The Belt and Road: Security dimensions. *Asia Europe Journal*, 16(3), 213–222.

China Daily. (2016 December 21), 5.

Cressey, D. R. (1997). The functions and structure of criminal syndicates. In Patrick Ryan and George E. Rush (eds.), *Understanding Organized Crime in Global Perspective: A Reader.* London: Sage Publications.

Criminal Code of the Republic of China. (2018). Retrieved from https://law.moj. gov.tw/ENG/LawClass/LawAll.aspx?pcode=C0000001.

Lo, S. S. (2009). *The Politics of Cross-Border Crime in Greater China.* New York: M.E. Sharpe.

Lo, S. S. (2018). *The Politics of Policing in Greater China.* London: Palgrave.

Lo, S. S., Hung, S. C. and Loo, J. H. (2019). *China's New United Front Work in Hong Kong: Penetrative Politics and its Implications.* London: Palgrave Macmillan.

Ming Pao. (2017 December 23), A11.

Mai, J. (2015 November 10). Hundreds arrested as police crack phone-scam gangs based overseas targeting Hong Kong, mainland China. *South China Morning Post.* Retrieved from https://www.scmp.com/news/hong-kong/law-crime/article/1877371/hundreds-arrested-police-crack-phone-scam-gangs-based.

Sing Tao Daily. (2018 April 21). A24.

Ta Kung Pao. (2018a February 23). A19.

Ta Kung Pao. (2018b October 27). A4.

Wen Wei Po. (2018 October 28). A1.

Chapter 12

Is the Belt and Road Initiative in Africa Sustainable?*

Francis C. Nwachukwu

School of Business, University of Saint Joseph, Macau, China

Abstract

In 2000, the China–Africa relationship was further strengthened with the establishment of the Forum on China–Africa Cooperation (FOCAC). The FOCAC offers a platform for consultation and cooperation mechanisms aimed at deepening diplomatic, security, trade and investment relations between China and African countries. Later came the Belt and Road Initiative (BRI) in 2013, an international trade network initiated by China that connects the three continents of Asia, Europe and Africa. The BRI focuses on the following key areas: cultural exchange; policy coordination; facilities connectivity; trade and investment; and financial integration. The BRI shares development objectives similar to those of the United Nations' Sustainable Development Goals (SDGs). In fact, the BRI implements part of the SDGs and provides a practical mechanism to strengthen the Sino-Africa relationship, which Africa can leverage to meet its Sustainable Goals. Africa is linked through the "Road" of the BRI plan and has received infrastructural projects funded by China to facilitate trade and integration of the national economies along the

---

*This chapter originally appeared in *Macau Ricci Institute Journal*, 2019, Issue 4, pp. 98–110.

trading route. Through the establishment of Economic and Trade Zones which attract investments from Chinese companies, and building infrastructures such as sea ports and railways, China through the BRI framework is helping Africa meet UN SGD Goal 9 concerning industry, innovation and infrastructure. A practical effect is that the BRI is helping African countries overcome the infrastructure gap, create jobs, acquire skills and promote integration between countries.

Is the Belt and Road Initiative in Africa Sustainable?

In 2013, China announced the Belt and Road Initiative (BRI) development strategy and in the same year, the United Nations announced its Sustainable Development Goals (SDGs) (Shah, 2016). The BRI encompasses two corridors — the Silk Road Economic Belt (referred to as "Belt") and the 21st century Maritime Silk Road (referred as "Road") (Figure 1). There are about 60 countries linked to the BRI trading route reaching about 63 percent of the global population and amounting to 29 percent of global GDP (Solmecke, 2016). China aims to build a trade

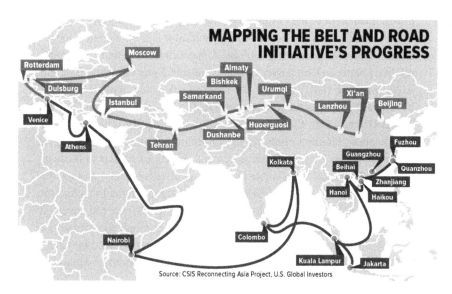

Figure 1.   The Belt and Road Routes (Yamada and Palma, 2018).

network that connects three continents — Asia, Europe, and Africa — while building land and maritime infrastructures that integrate the economies of the countries on the trading routes (Shah, 2016; Solmecke, 2016). In Africa, beyond the massive BRI projects that capture most attention are the growing investments from Chinese entrepreneurs. According to Feng and Pilling (2019), the volume of Chinese investments in Africa was 2 percent of the US level in 2000, rose to 55 percent of that level in 2014, and now is on track within a decade to surpass the US levels. There is increasing Chinese presence in Africa, which is evidence of growing Sino-Africa relations. Africa's inclusion in BRI opens opportunities for development projects and investments from China which may enable Africa to meet its 2030 Agenda for a socially fair, prosperous and secure environment.

The Belt and Road Initiative

The Silk Road Economic Belt was announced by the Chinese president Xi Jinping in 2013 at Nazarbayev University in Kazakhstan. A month later in October of the same year Xi announced the 21st Century Maritime Silk Road during a speech at the Indonesian parliament (Solmecke, 2016). The historic "Silk Road" which dates before the Common Era (BCE) highlights organized trade and exchange among peoples whose caravans travelled the long-range trade routes starting from the cities of the Middle Kingdom (present-day China) such as Dalian, Xiamen, Tianjin, Guangzhou, Wuhan, Shanghai and many more, through the countries of Central Asia to the ancient Persian Empire and onto Europe (Etemad, 2016). The caravans carried their goods on camels or horses and made stops at designated locations called "*Caravanserai*" to rest, re-stock food and water and set off again till they reach a trading city where goods were exchanged through barter (Etemad, 2016). The BRI seeks to reestablish the historical Silk Road characterized by the caravan traders now using modern transportation systems, building upon new or upgraded infrastructures to support the integration of the BRI countries (Shah, 2016).

The 21st century Maritime Silk Road corridor is a maritime route that links China with South and Southeast Asia, with connections to East and North Africa and Europe. The "Road" encompasses seas and oceans such as the South China Sea, Indian Ocean, Arabian Sea, Strait of Malacca, Red Sea, Persian Gulf and Gulf of Bengal. Although the "Belt" offers new

Figure 2.   UN 17 Sustainable Development Goals (United Nations, n.d.).

possibilities, the volume of transport and the costs of overland travel make the maritime "Road" an indispensable component to China's foreign trade. China's geostrategic objective is to reduce dependence on the Malacca Strait, which carries over 90 percent of China's seaborne trade, and to guarantee an uninterrupted supply of raw materials (Koboević, Kurtela, and Vujičić, 2018).

Referred to as the "Malacca Dilemma", China considers it risky to rely exclusively on the Straits of Malacca, and is addressing this risk by building ports in the Indian Ocean Region (IOR), as in Sri Lanka, Pakistan, Bangladesh and Myanmar (Koboević *et al.*, 2018). China is also building

> The BRI ushers in a different form of China's engagement with Africa in which a core objective is to promote trade through investments and building infrastructures.

transport infrastructures essential to enhance maximum use of these port facilities. The BRI projects will facilitate China's international trade cooperation, and aim to create the world's largest platform promoting trade, financial collaboration, and social and cultural cooperation among countries on the trade route.

Sustainability of Belt and Road in Africa

The 2030 Agenda for the United Nations' Sustainable Development Goals (SDGs) was adopted by world leaders at the UN Summit in September 2015, and came into effect on January 1, 2016 (United Nations, n.d.) (Figure 2). The 17 SDGs aim globally to achieve economic growth, social inclusion and environmental sustainability. For African countries, achieving the UN SDGs requires a rethinking of economic policies and new partnerships with development agencies and the private sector. Africa's heretofore insignificant contribution to global trade stems from inadequate infrastructure, skills and lack of capacity for production. To reduce poverty and enhance Africa's competitiveness in global trade would require Africans to adopt a local development model that maximizes their national resources. The abundance of human and natural resources when properly harnessed will support Africa's sustainable development. To this end Africa is in need of a cooperative development model that is supportive of the UN's SDGs. China has the potential to help Africa fulfill its needs. The BRI provides a framework to enhance a strategic partnership between China and Africa that fosters socio-economic cooperation. During a visit to South Africa by President Xi, the Forum of China–Africa Cooperation pledged "(to) actively explore the linkages between China's initiatives of building the Silk Road Economic Belt and 21st Century Maritime Silk Road and Africa's economic integration and sustainable development agenda" (Chen, 2018). Given China's interest in promoting the BRI, Africa should leverage the opportunities to meet its strategic needs.

Africa is in dire need of infrastructural development (Leke, Chironga, and Desvaux, 2018). China is funding infrastructure projects and investments that have long-term economic impact and this is crucial for Africa's sustainable development. Some of the existing infrastructure in Africa was built during the colonial era and is mostly dilapidated with little or no maintenance or modernization, making continued operation increasingly difficult. Issues that affect Africa's infrastructural development stem from a lack of political will to initiate modern projects to keep up with needs arising from urbanization, compounded by forms of corruption which leave projects either with bloated costs or in some cases abandoned. The consequence is that Africa has not performed well in either intra-African trade or trade with the world, due to difficulties encountered in transporting goods and services (Ubi, 2018).

The BRI ushers in a different form of China's engagement with Africa in which a core objective is to promote trade through investments and building infrastructures. Africa's urbanization is growing rapidly and predicted to be the fastest in the world (Leke *et al.*, 2018). Chinese backed infrastructural projects and capacity building will help Africa build and maintain infrastructure needed to meet the pressure from urbanization.

Here are some examples of BRI-related projects in Africa:

The BRI-linked projects in Table 1 have helped East African countries achieve UN SDG Goal 9 which targets investments in infrastructures and Goal 11 which targets provision of transport and basic services to all. The Ethiopia–Djibouti electrified railway provides both passenger and freight services connecting landlocked Ethiopia to the port of Djibouti. The Kenyan Madaraka Express, a standard gauge rail connecting the capital Nairobi to Mombasa, cut the travel time by more than half, offering an alternative to a bumpy bus ride on potholed highways that have caused fatal accidents (Sow, 2017). These projects are financed by loans and, with mounting debt issues, there are risks of debt sustainability and an inability by governments to address other social needs due to limited funding. Nevertheless, the projects do have positive social impact, especially in the area of transport and trade.

Djibouti has attracted major infrastructure BRI-linked projects as a result of its strategic location, such as a multipurpose port, Free Trade Zone, China telecoms data center and the location for China's first-ever overseas naval base (Chen, 2018). The Chinese commercial and military

Table 1.   BRI Projects in East Africa (Chen, 2018; Sow, 2017; *Xinhua*, 2018).

Ethiopia	Addis-Djibouti SGR	US$4 billion loan financed by China Exim bank
Kenya	Nairobi–Mombasa Madaraka Express	US$3.2 billion loan financed by China Exim bank (with rail network plans to Uganda, Democratic Republic of Congo, Rwanda, Burundi, South Sudan and Ethiopia)
Djibouti	Doraleh Multipurpose Port	US$294 million loan financed by China Exim bank
Djibouti	Damerjog Livestock Port	US$51 million loan financed by China Exim bank
Djibouti	Multipurpose Free Trade Zone	US$150 million credit from China Merchants

interests in Djibouti provide socio-economic development benefits and counter-piracy operations in the Gulf of Aden.

Key Elements and Challenges

The BRI addresses China's strategic interests such as building an extensive trade network for exporting its products. It is also in China's interest to have a diversified network of land and sea routes that guarantee an adequate supply of resources. On the African side, however, there are cases where

> There is a concern regarding the sustainability of these debt-based projects. Debts must be repaid and as interest mounts, money used for debt servicing could have been used for other development projects.

countries embark on projects without due diligence that may result in negative consequences thereby eroding the initial benefit to the government. For example, Figure 3 shows the Bagamoyo Special Economic

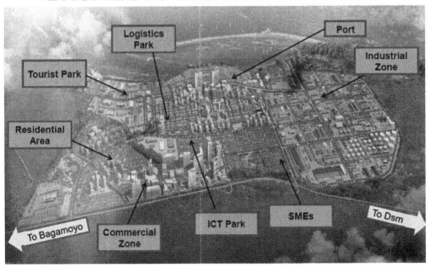

Figure 3.   Bagamoyo Special Economic Zone (Barnes, 2014).

Zone (SEZ), a US$10 billion project in Tanzania in partnership with China and Oman signed in 2013 (Tairo, 2017). Since the Tanzanian government was unable to fulfill its own commitment to the project, valued at US$28 million, it will proceed with China Merchants Holdings International (CMHI) financing the shortfall. The consequence is that the Tanzanian government will lose its ownership stake and the benefits that accrue to this long-term project. It may not be in the national interest of Tanzania to cede to a Chinese entity the complete ownership of such a gigantic project with huge economic potential. The Bagamoyo Port when completed will be the largest in East Africa and is expected to start operation between 2020 and 2021.

Benefits of BRI-Linked Investments

The BRI is intended to increase the integration of different countries and boost economic growth. This offers China a market access opportunity to export its goods and internationalize Chinese infrastructure firms — an opportunity to offshore excess capacity (Chen, 2018). Some of the benefits include:

- Industrial capacity — Chinese companies influenced by the BRI are establishing business operations in African countries. These companies will improve the industrial capacity of African products with spillover effects on employment, capacity building and balance of trade.
- Infrastructure — Africa is in need of infrastructural development. BRI projects, such as ports and railways, will boost infrastructure. Some of the ongoing BRI projects have been previously conceived by African governments due to their socio-economic benefits but paucity of funds affected execution. China through the BRI is supporting African countries with finance to execute the projects. The rail network in East Africa financed by China will integrate the countries within the region and facilitate movement of people, goods, and services.
- Economic growth — Both industrial capacity and improved infrastructure contribute to economic growth. Local manufacturing with an efficient network of transport facilities connected to the port will facilitate trade. BRI-financed industrial parks, railways, roads, and ports will boost economic activities.

Challenges

The BRI has also brought to Africa its own level of fears and concerns, such as:

- Trade imbalance — without a clear strategy, African countries will have little leverage to balance trade with China. Financing major infrastructure projects gives China a competitive edge during trade negotiations. African markets will continue to witness an influx of Chinese goods as opening market access may be a precondition for China to finance projects.
- Rising Debt — a majority of BRI-linked projects in Africa are supported by loans or debt-based financing (see Table 1). There is a concern regarding the sustainability of these debt-based projects. Debts must be repaid and as interest mounts, money used for debt servicing could have been used for other development projects. There is also a concern regarding the consequences of default, as China takes over the projects when the loans cannot be repaid. For African nations this emerges as a national security issue for long-term infrastructure projects.
- Environment — projects such as ports, railways, and industrial parks affect local communities and may create negative environmental consequences. An awareness of climate change should be factored in while initiating these projects. Such a priority is in accordance with the UN SDG Goals, which give appropriate attention to environmental sustainability. African governments and Chinese companies should be guided by the UN Goals, to ensure projects have a positive impact on the host communities in the long run.
- Impact — there is a need to ensure that BRI projects are strategically aligned with Chinese economic and political interests. Proper assessment is required to ensure these projects will positively impact the economy of the receiving countries and should not increase the potential for corruption by government officials. Africa is in great need of infrastructural development, economic transformation, and cutting-edge technologies. Projects that respond to these needs will enhance sustainable development. Adequate compensation may be negotiated fairly and effectively to minimize the problems of affected communities, including appropriate and timely resettlement schemes. Most importantly, the BRI projects should connect national economies and

boost economic growth and development that are mutually beneficial to both China and African countries.

Conclusion

The Belt and Road Initiative provides an opportunity which African countries can leverage to contribute towards the 2030 Agenda for Sustainable Development Goals. The SDGs require international cooperation and collaboration with the private sector to achieve these goals. As China deepens investments and development projects in Africa, there is a need to keep abreast of the social and economic impact of these projects towards sustainable development, deepen mutual understanding through cross-cultural exchanges, ensure no corruption, and ensure environmental protection and the enforcement of acceptable labor standards.

References

Barnes, R. (2014). Construction of Bagamoyo port finally set to start off in 2015. Retrieved from https://constructionreviewonline.com/2014/10/construction-bagamoyo-port-finally-set-start-2015/.

Chen, Y. (2018). Silk Road to the Sahel: African ambitions in China's Belt and Road Initiative. Policy Brief. China Africa Research Initiative, 4.

Etemad, H. (2016). International entrepreneurship as a young field of scholarly inquiry and its relationship with the knowledge network of five related disciplines. *Journal of International Entrepreneurship*, 14(2), 157–167. (n.d./2018). Doi:10.1007/ s10843-016-0180-1.

Koboević, Ž., Kurtela, Ž., and Vujičić, S. (2018). The Maritime Silk Road and China's Belt and Road Initiative. *Pomorski Put Svile i Kineska Inicijativa "pojas i Put"*, 65(2), 113–122. (n.d. / 2018). Doi:10.17818/NM/2018/2.7.

Leke, A., Chironga, M., and Desvaux, G. (2018). The overlooked revolution for business in Africa | McKinsey. Retrieved from https://www.mckinsey.com/featured-insights/middle-east-and-africa/africas-overlooked-business-revolution.

Feng, E. and Pilling, D. (2019, March 27). The other side of Chinese investment in Africa. *Financial Times*. Retrieved from https://www.ft.com/content/9f5736d8-14e1-11e9-a581-4ff78404524e.

Shah, A. (2016). Building a sustainable 'Belt and Road.' Retrieved from http://www.cirsd.org/en/horizons/horizons-spring-2016--issue-no-7/building-a-sustainable-%E2%80%98belt-and-road.

Solmecke, U. (2016). Multinational enterprises and the "one belt, one road" initiative: Sustainable development and innovation in a post-crisis global environment. *Copenhagen Journal of Asian Studies*, 34(2), 9–27.

Sow, M. (2017). Africa in the news: Kenya inaugurates its first high-speed railway, Barclays sells Africa shares, and Zuma survives no confidence vote. Retrieved from https://www.brookings.edu/blog/africa-in-focus/2017/06/02/africa-in-the-news-kenya-inaugurates-its-first-high-speed-railway-barclays-sells-africa-shares-and-zuma-survives-no-confidence-vote/.

Tairo, A. (2017). Dar surrenders Bagamoyo port project to Chinese. Retrieved from https://www.theeastafrican.co.ke/business/Tanzania-Bagamoyo-port-project-to-Chinese/2560-4122244- rxa9wtz/index.html.

Ubi, E. (2018). Africa's need for infrastructure to fast-track development. Financial Nigeria International Limited. Retrieved from http://www.financialnigeria.com/africa-s-need-for-infrastructure-to-fast-track-development-blog-391.html.

United Nations. (n.d.). The sustainable development agenda. Retrieved from https://www.un.org/sustainabledevelopment/development-agenda/.

Xinhua. (2018). Chinese-built Ethiopia-Djibouti railway begins commercial operations — *Xinhua | English.news.cn.* Retrieved from http://www.xinhuanet.com/english/2018-01/01/c_136865306.htm.

Yamada, G. and Palma, S. (2018). Is China's Belt and Road working? Retrieved from https://reconnectingasia.csis.org/analysis/entries/is-china-belt-and-road-working/.

Chapter 13

The Belt and Road Initiative: Opportunities and Challenges*

Mike Thompson

*Adjunct Professor, Gustavson School of Business,
University of Victoria and Director of the Anthesis Academy,
Anthesis Group*

Abstract

This paper begins by setting out the vision for the renaissance of the New Silk Road as the "Belt and Road Initiative" (BRI) announced by President Xi Jinping in 2013 and picks out a theme of moral leadership in Xi's speeches. The opportunities for a Chinese approach to the Common Good are contrasted with six major challenges to Xi's aspirations for the BRI as a pathway leading to friendship, shared development and peace. The Silk Road has a rich history across Asian civilizations with earliest records of it dating from the Han dynasty (207 BCE–220 CE). Over the centuries, the Silk Road has not only opened up a path for trade with silk as currency but also great opportunities for cross-cultural understanding and relations. The Silk Road has provided a means for the transmission of art, science, cultural and religious exchange. The BRI essentially promotes a regenerated Silk Road of infrastructural connectivity within and across China's borders. It brings together the "Silk

---

*This chapter originally appeared in *Macau Ricci Institute Journal*, 2019, Issue 4, pp. 15–28.

Road Economic Belt" of roads, railways and industrial corridors and the "21st Century Maritime Silk Road", expanding through upgraded ports. The BRI extends beyond ports, railways and highways to other major types of infrastructure including oil and gas pipelines, electricity power plants and telecommunications networks. Construction of the $68 billion China–Pakistan Economic Corridor creates a major highway running from the deep-water port of Gwadar in Pakistan to the city of Kashgar in the Xinjiang region of China, improving connectivity between the two countries and offering central and western China more direct access to the Indian Ocean and the Arabian Sea. Projects are also underway in several of the other corridors. As the Center for Strategic and International Studies (CSIS) has pointed out, the BRI is "more of a sweeping vision" than "an operational blueprint", though it is far more credible and tangible than skeptics might like to believe (Johnson, 2016). A starting point for this enquiry inevitably begins with the plans originally set out by President Xi Jinping and China's State Council in 2015. This paper aims to report Xi's comments as an observer rather than as a critic following Watson (1994) to overcome externally imposed meaning and to appreciate other people's realities.

Positive Opportunities

Ethical dilemmas inevitably arise in the midst of conflicts of geo-political interest, rival commercial interests and a multitude of conflicting personal interests for both wealth creation and personal prestige and advancement. The conflicts of the human condition are simply given a new road on which to travel and potentially exploit those who are poorer and less powerful: prosperity for the few potentially at the expense of the many. But is it reasonable to question the central intent of President Xi in pointing not only to the rejuvenation of the Chinese nation in expanding global trade but in helping peoples in small nations in SE Asia and Africa to develop?

The Chinese government envisages BRI countries working in concert to secure an efficient network of land, sea and air passages; lifting their connectivity to a higher level; enhancing trade and investment facilitation; establishing a network of free trade areas that meet high standards; maintaining closer economic ties; deepening political trust; enhancing cultural exchanges; encouraging different peoples to learn from each other and flourish together (*NDRC*, 2015). The overarching moral claim put forward at the outset was that the BRI would promote mutual understanding, peace and friendship among peoples of all countries. President Xi has explained this claim within his five guiding principles of the BRI:

1. A road for peace: "The ancient silk routes thrived in times of peace, but lost vigour in times of war".
2. A road of prosperity: "Development holds the master key to solving all problems.... Infrastructure connectivity is the foundation of development through cooperation".
3. A road of opening up: "Opening up brings progress while isolation results in backwardness [...] We should build an open platform of cooperation and uphold and grow an open world economy".
4. A road of innovation: "We should pursue innovation-driven development and intensify cooperation in frontier areas such as digital economy, artificial intelligence, nanotechnology, and quantum computing [...] we should pursue the new vision of green development [...]".
5. A road connecting different civilizations: "We should ensure that when it comes to different civilisations, exchange will replace estrangement, mutual learning will replace clashes, and coexistence will replace a sense of superiority" (Xi, 2017a).

Although the focus of BRI action by business and political elites is on the infrastructural, commercial and trade opportunities, there is an "other-interested" intent made explicit by Xi: "If we take the first courageous step towards each other, we can embark on a path leading to friendship, shared development, peace, harmony and a better future" (Xi, 2017a).

These ideals point towards a vision for the Common Good and, more precisely the "internal goods of excellence" (MacIntyre, 1983) cultivated through cooperative activity and social practice: truthfulness, justice, courage and humility. But operationalizing the Common Good requires that the "goods of effectiveness" achievable through market activity presuppose the regulation of agency relationships and asymmetric power relations, restrained by controls that promote distributive justice and backed by Party disciplinary oversight and penalties. Economic opportunism by Belt and Road players on all sides could lead to monopolistic and monopsonist practices that contradict Xi's intent for the BRI to become a path of friendship and cooperation amongst nations.

Xi's five guiding principles demand that the benefits of infrastructural connectivity are led with responsibility, accountability and justice despite the turmoil of geo-political tensions and disputes. The ideals of shared development, peace and harmony are realized through the principle of friendship. The demand is for leadership with character and virtue to fulfill Xi's vision of the BRI as a path to friendship. The high challenge of virtuous friendship is not based on the mutually beneficial outcomes of reciprocity assumed by Xi, but by a willing acceptance of responsibility for the other. For China as the leading player in the BRI, the virtues of humility and generosity are indispensable for achieving Xi's hope that "coexistence will replace a sense of superiority".

Geopolitical Dilemmas

Competitive spheres of influence over regions along the BRI are inevitable. Conflict can rapidly overtake cooperation especially when debts to China cannot be repaid. A number of commentators such as the Center for Global Development (Starrs, 2018) have pointed out the risk of debt bondage in future BRI financing and list eight countries that face a "high risk of debt distress". Sri Lanka owes $8 billion in debt to Chinese state firms which upgraded Sri Lanka's ports and other maritime facilities. Desperate for debt relief Sri Lanka handed over the China-funded Port of Hambantota on a 99-year lease. In similar circumstances, China has taken a 40-year lease on one of Pakistan's most important ports (Kurlantzick, 2018).

So far, according to Du and Zhang's study, BRI participating countries "have been cooperative with Chinese acquirers, probably thanks to the high-profile international political cooperation feature embedded in the OBOR initiative" (Du and Zhang, 2018). A major research study on China's outward foreign direct investment (OFDI) by Li, Luo and De Vita (2018) suggests that Chinese investors are influenced more by the difference of the institutional environment between China and the host

---

For China as the leading player in the BRI, the virtues of humility and generosity are indispensable for achieving Xi's hope that "coexistence will replace a sense of superiority".

---

country than government intervention. This finding highlights the economic advantage of respect and cooperation between China and the country receiving OFDI for the success of the BRI. Du and Zhang (2018) provide evidence on the efficiency and efficacy of the state capitalist system in promoting international economic integration through both SOE acquirers and non-SOE acquirers.

The potential for geopolitical dilemmas is illustrated in the case of Australia where headlines, news reports and opinion pieces have, in the words of Laurenceson, given rise to "China Threat, China Angst and China Panic" (Laurenceson, 2018, p. 5). Resource-rich Papua New Guinea (PNG), a former Australian colony, is a current focus of the tensions between China and the Australian government. China and Australia are both eager to exploit PNG's natural gas, minerals and timber resources. In January 2018, Australia launched a scathing attack on China's efforts to build influence in the Pacific, accusing Beijing of currying favor with the region's smaller nations by funneling cash into little-used infrastructure projects. According to Concetta Fierravanti-Wells, Australia's minister for international development and the Pacific, "You've got the Pacific full of these useless buildings which nobody maintains, which are basically white elephants" (Wembridge, 2018). Zheng Zeguang, China's vice-minister of foreign affairs, responded by explaining how China was "just making the cake of co-operation larger" (Hornby and Smyth, 2018). From Papua New Guinea's perspective, China is a friend who builds infrastructure and gives social support in the form of a medical team to prevent the spread of malaria, a "friendship school" and disaster relief and reconstruction following a recent earthquake (Ge, 2018, p. 1). Despite the Australian federal government's position, Victoria's premier, Daniel Andrews, signed a Belt and Road agreement in October 2018 which he said would "provide an impetus for pushing forward Victoria's cooperation with China" (Jinxi, 2018).

The Challenges of the Belt and Road Initiative

Managing peaceful relations with a rising power

Xi's agenda for cooperation and independence is difficult to manage with justice when power relations are unequal. Inevitably questions of China's asymmetric power are raised. Western media commentators do not readily accept Xi's promise that "coexistence will replace a sense of superiority" but the widespread concern that smaller nations are overpowered by Chinese money and infrastructural connectivity is not readily supported by the evidence. In 2018, Malaysia announced that it would renegotiate its contracts with China, describing them as "unequal treaties" and a "new version of colonialism". The Maldives, Myanmar, Pakistan, and Sierra Leone are reviewing the scale and scope of their cooperation with China (Roland, 2019). In contrast The Philippines, a significant recipient of Chinese state and private investment, has not enforced a decision reached by an international tribunal in 2016 that upheld Manila's South China Sea claims. Of course, cooperation can work positively both ways and Xi's recent call to negotiate a free trade agreement with Pacific Island nations promises a significant economic benefit (Baijie, 2018).

Apart from the extension of soft power and geopolitical influence advantages there are a number of security and economic prizes to be secured for China through the BRI: energy security, development of Chinese eastern provinces and growth for infrastructural exports (Leavy, 2018, p. 37). According to India's *Economic Times*, perhaps the biggest unnamed prize would be to put China back where it once was, at the center of the global economy. The side effect is likely to increase the dependency on China for the tools of economic development: steel, construction, infrastructure, technology and finance.

China's hope is that by bolstering growth in recipient nations, "the initiative could also win over hearts and minds, convincing people in those countries that China's rise as regional hegemon will, overall, benefit them too" (Kurlantzic, 2018). Nevertheless, the moral leadership challenge lies with China to bolster global security and to contain the "rejuvenation of the Chinese nation" peacefully to fulfill Xi's aim for the BRI to "open more cooperation channels" (Xi, 2017a).

Managing financialization and anticorruption

The BRI ambitions may conflict with the powerful drives of financialization[1] in which spontaneous and over-optimistic assessments can dominate decision-making and lead to corrupt and rent-seeking practices. The negative effects of financialization have been portrayed by the Pontifical Council for Justice and Peace as "Business leaders increasingly focus on

---

[1] In 2015, the Pontifical Council published *The Vocation of the Business Leader* in which it pointed to the financialization of the world economy as having deleterious effects and defining financialization as "the shift in the capitalist economy from production to finance. The revenue and profits of the financial sector have become an increasingly large segment of the world-wide economy" (Pontifical Council, 2015, p. 9).

maximizing wealth, employees develop attitudes of entitlement, and consumers demand instant gratification at the lowest possible price" (Pontifical Council, 2015, p. 3).

The high aims of Xi's principles require behaviors, practices, enforceable law-making and regulatory scrutiny to manage the ever-present moral hazards of selfishness beyond self- interest that are present in all of us and all along the Belt and Road. The fatal attractions of wealth and power have led government officials and business people to do bad things.

> If the language of friendship is mounted on a narrow platform of investment and infrastructural connectivity then friendship is not an end but a means to achieve self-interested objectives which prioritize power, capital and influence.

The Chinese transformation of the village of Khorgos in Kazakhstan to an inland shipping hub and free trade zone highlights the ethical blowback of local-level smuggling and high-profile corruption cases. Khorgos also illustrates the plight that can face workers in BRI projects as reported by Mauk (2019):

> While new official jobs in Khorgos are lifting a lucky few out of poverty, it is far more common to find farmers and herders moonlighting as taxi drivers, security guards or smugglers, part of a precarious network of low-paid freelancers. Such work is susceptible by design to sudden changes in enforcement and depends on a constant influx of disposable workers. It seemed like a high cost for connecting the world.

In light of such stories, at the Belt and Road Symposium in August 2018, Xi gave explicit instruction to the Party to strengthen its moral leadership and oversight of Chinese companies operating overseas to ensure that their behavior and practices reflected well on projects that are "worthy of praise". BRI projects should "improve the global governance system" and bring forth a "community of shared destiny" (Rolland, 2019).

Managing conflicting views of justice and cooperation

For the BRI to be "a road with high ethical standards" there will need to be just and trusted arbitration mechanisms alongside the gestures for harmony and peace. Strategic rivalries and the commercial exploitation of people and natural resources are ever-present dangers. Governments and companies are increasingly under pressure to work out the principles of distributive justice, such that the "larger cake of cooperation" is shared to reduce inequality, protect workers and preserve natural resources and ecosystems. China plans to set up international courts in Shenzhen and Xi'an to resolve BRI commercial disputes. Whether such courts will be based on true independency is under question (Kuo and Kommenda, 2018).

In 2017 President Xi offered strong and measurable goals for projects supporting social and poverty alleviation in countries along the Belt and Road over a three-year period with assistance worth RMB 60 billion to developing countries and international organizations (Xi, 2017a). In 2018 Xi called for small-scale projects that responded to the immediate needs of local populations and not just the elites and for more people-to-people exchanges (Rolland, 2018).

Strategic rivalries all involve a degree of self-interest but the emphasis of the BRI message is "win-win" and friendship. The message is being tested as China's major state-owned enterprises attempt to build relationships and navigate cross-cultural challenges before any deals are signed. For example, CRRC, China's railway enterprise, has invested heavily in a five-year educational program for senior executives to learn about international business, law, governance and finance. Intrinsic to this kind of education is the basic need to respect the rights of different peoples and to better understand the values that underpin a company's stakeholder relations and its ethical, social and environmental corporate responsibilities.

Advancing local educational development

The demand for talent and innovation at the financial and technological frontiers of the Belt and Road inevitably attracts Chinese talent and skills. But how might such talent and skills be nurtured within the local communities of the Belt and Road? No plan is clear. The promise of RMB 60 billion funding for BRI social projects could be prioritized to ensure support for long-term strategic educational development capacity planning at the weakest points along the Belt and Road. Educational projects could be designed to stem the cycles of social deprivation caused by a lack of educational resources in developing countries.

Despite talk of educational cooperation by Beijing there is no evidence of an educational resource plan within the BRI to further educational advancement in parallel with economic advancement. For example, the Second Belt and Road Education Dialogue held in Beijing in November 2018 discussed educational exchanges as means of support for the BRI rather than the BRI becoming a means of support for educational advancement in other countries.

Managing cross-cultural understanding despite the fears that China will dominate

A country's social and cultural influence, many Chinese companies, particularly inexperienced ones, struggle with local cultures and politics (O'Meara, 2018). Economic exchange needs to be accompanied by social and cultural exchange to build trust, mutual understanding and the peaceful outcomes enshrined in Xi's five principles. Sino-Russian relations are an example of improved cross-cultural understanding. China has opened over twenty Confucius Institutes and Confucius Classrooms in Russia. But the cross-cultural relationship is tied to the economic relationship. For example, China has increased its debt financing of Russian companies as a result of Western sanctions against Russia.

It is in cross-cultural understanding that we can learn from the early mission work of the Jesuits in the 16th and 17th centuries following the example of the friendship of Matteo Ricci and Paul Xu Guangqi who engaged with the Confucian intellectual elite literati to establish a spiritual dialogue with Chinese scholars. In the context of friendship, they introduced Western science, mathematics, cartography, astronomy and the visual arts to the imperial court. The missionaries recognized the inspiration of Confucian wisdom as well as sharing the treasures of their own faith. Chinese aspirations for peaceful cooperation are threatened by financialization of the road without a quality of empathetic dialogue between different people and religious groups who lie along the Belt and Road. If the language of friendship is mounted on a narrow platform of investment and infrastructural connectivity then friendship is not an end but a means to achieve self-interested objectives which prioritize power, capital and influence.

True collaboration will respect cultural and religious difference, promote reciprocity as shown by the nature of friendship between Catholic and Protestant missionaries and the Chinese. The work of the Ricci Institutes continues this tradition today believing that inter-religious dialogue and an appreciation of the spiritual traditions of Buddhism, Confucianism, Islam and Daoism offer the means to open up the minds and souls of people from every nation and culture to the betterment of humankind.

The challenge and the opportunity are to promote cross-cultural and inter-religious encounters for the Common Good beyond institutionalized one-way communication.

Managing cross-border data flows

According to Meltzer and Lovelock, governments restrict cross-border data flows to:

- Protect or improve citizens' personal privacy;
- Ensure rapid access to data by law enforcement officials;
- Protect or ensure national security;
- Improve economic growth or economic competitiveness;
- Level the regulatory playing field (Meltzer and Lovelock, 2018, p. v).

Ensuring data privacy is a shared concern — but how far can cross-border data flows really be checked? According to Adam Segal of the Council on Foreign Relations, "cyberspace will be much less American and much more Chinese" and Beijing is likely to have its biggest impact on global Internet governance through its trade and investment policies, especially as part of the BRI (Segal, 2018).

For companies from countries outside China who engage in joint-venture projects with Chinese partners the 2017 Cyber Security Law (CSL) is, according to the specialist risk consultancy Control Risks, causing deep concern for the management of data. They point to the extensive Party controls on network content that require opening up their IT systems:

The growing chokehold over information flows and the technology that delivers it is pushing foreign MNCs in China either to be "all in" or to reevaluate their operations in China, as a whole. This means IT personnel, operations and data specialists, procuring domestic technology, and localizing IT security policies, content and crisis management plans (Kedl and Wilford, 2018).

The likely impact of these policies is to prevent the BRI moving into North America, Europe, Australia and New Zealand. But other countries along the Belt and Road in Africa and East Asia are not as sensitized to the control of data and network content. Global businesses generally welcome the digital Silk Road recognizing that data need to flow freely across borders to scale and create value, and to fight against governments that require local data storage. China will be at the center of such battles with its current data localization laws.

Conclusion

Xi's speeches on the BRI point to sharing economic and developmental benefits but also of principles of moral leadership as part of an integrated shared value proposition. He argues that the BRI is a positive good, especially to those "countries who want to speed up their development while preserving their independence; and it offers Chinese wisdom and a Chinese approach to solving the problems facing mankind" (Xi, 2017b). From moral leadership and comparative spirituality perspectives China is attempting to share its rich wisdom heritage. Xi's apparent desire to avoid imposing Sinicization needs to be matched by a reciprocity of engagement in East–West wisdom resources to create the kind of moral leadership that could enable the BRI to be a road of peace and true connectivity across different civilizations.

References

Du, J. and Zhang, Y. (2018). Does One Belt One Road initiative promote Chinese overseas direct investment? *China Economic Review*, 47, 189–205.

Ge, H. (2018). China, PNG to upgrade partnership. *Global Times*, pp. 1–2.

Hajari, N. (2018). View: Who should be afraid of the Belt and Road? *The Economic Times*. Retrieved from https://economictimes.indiatimes.com/news/international/world-news/view-who-should-be-afraid-of-the-belt-and-road-china.

Hamel, G. (2012). *What Matters Now*. San Francisco, CA: Jossey-Bass.

Hornby, L. and Smyth, J. (2018). China-Australia rivalry heats up over Pacific Islands. *Financial Times*. Retrieved from https://www.ft.com/content/6a2e1e2c-e7f5-11e8-8a85-04b8afea6ea3.

Jinxi, M. (2018). Australian state signs cooperation agreement on Belt, Road Initiative. *China Daily Europe.* Retrieved from http://europe.chinadaily.com. cn/a/201810/31/WS5bd8f4e7a310eff3032858ec.html.

Johnson, C. (2016). President Xi Jinping's "Belt and Road" initiative: A practical assessment of the Chinese Communist Party's roadmap for China's global resurgence. *A Report of the CSIS Freeman Chair in China Studies.* Center for Strategic and International Studies (CSIS).

Kedl, K. and Wilford, S. (2018). Future-proofing your China strategy and business operations. Control Risks. Retrieved from https://www.controlrisks. com/campaigns/china-business/future-proofing-your-china-strategy.

Kuo, L and Kommenda, N. (2018). What is China's Belt and Road initiative? *The Guardian.* Retrieved from https://www.theguardian.com/cities/ng-interactive/2018/jul/30/what-china-belt-road-initiative-silk-road-explainer.

Kurlantzick, J. (2018). China's risky play for global power. *Washington Monthly.* September/October. Retrieved from https://washingtonmonthly.com/ magazine/september-october-2018/chinas-risky-play-for-global-power.

Laurenceson, J. (2018). *Do the Claims Stack Up? Australia Talks China.* Broadway NSW: Australia-China Relations Institute (ACRI).

Leavy, B. (2018). China's "New Silk Road" initiative — implications for competitors and partners, near and far. *Strategy & Leadership*, 46(2), 34–40.

Li, C., Luo, Y. and De Vita, G. (2018). Institutional difference and outward FDI: Evidence from China. *Empirical Economics.* Doi: 10.1007/s00181-018-1564-y.

MacIntyre, A. (1983). *After Virtue: A Study in Moral Theory.* London: Bloomsbury.

Mauk, B. (2019). Can China turn the middle of nowhere into the center of the world economy? *The New York Times Magazine.* Retrieved from https:// www.nytimes.com/interactive/2019/01/29/magazine/china-globalization-kazakhstan.html.

Meltzer, J. and Lovelock, P. (2018). Regulating for a digital economy: Understanding the importance of cross-border data flows in Asia. Global Economy and Development at Brookings.

National Development and Reform Commission (NDRC). (2015). Vision and actions on jointly building silk road economic belt and 21st-century maritime silk road. Retrieved from http://en.ndrc.gov.cn/newsrelease/201503/ t20150330_669367.html.

O'Meara, S. (2018). Taking the silk road to high-tech growth. *Nature.* Retrieved from https://www.nature.com/articles/d41586-018-07202-6.

Pence, M. (2018). Apec summit: Mike Pence warns of China's 'constricting belt' and 'one-way road'. *The Guardian.* Retrieved from https://www.theguardian. com/world/2018/nov/18/apec-summit-mike-pence-warns-of-chinas-constricting-belt-and-one-way-road.

Pontifical Council for Justice and Peace. (2015). *Vocation of the Business Leader.* Rome.

Rolland, N. (2019). Reports of Belt and Road's death are greatly exaggerated. *Foreign Affairs.* Retrieved from https://www.foreignaffairs.com/articles/ china/2019-01-29/reports-belt-and-roads-death-are-greatly-exaggerated.

Segal, A. (2018). When China rules the web. *Foreign Affairs.* September/October. Retrieved from https://www.foreignaffairs.com/articles/china/2018-08-13/ when-china-rules-web.

Starrs, S. K. (2018). Belt and Road Initiative is no selfless venture. *Financial Times.* Retrieved from https://www.ft.com/content/098d85c4-9a6d-11e8-ab77-f854c65a4465.

Watson, T. J. (1994). *In Search of Management: Culture, Chaos, and Control in Managerial Work.* London: Routledge.

Wembridge, M. (2018). Australia lashes out at China's 'useless' Pacific projects. *Financial Times.* Retrieved from https://www.ft.com/content/9bd0cb6a-f5a6-11e7-8715-e94187b3017e.

Xi, J. (2017a). Work together to build the silk road economic belt, and the 21st century maritime silk road. *Xin Hua* speech given at the opening ceremony of The Belt and Road Forum for International Cooperation. Retrieved from http://www.xinhuanet.com/english/2017-05/14/c_136282982.htm.

Xi, J. (2017b). Socialism with Chinese characteristics enters new era: Xi. *China Daily.* Retrieved from http://www.chinadaily.com.cn/china/19thcpcnationalc ongress/2017-10/18/content_33398070.htm.

Index